Down to Earth

Also by Anne Scott-James

IN THE MINK
SISSINGHURST

Down to Earth

ANNE SCOTT-JAMES

with drawings by Osbert Lancaster

BLOOMSBURY

BLOOMSBURY GARDENING CLASSICS

Editorial Advisory Board

Montagu Don
Peter King

First published in Great Britain in 1971 by Michael Joseph Ltd.
This paperback edition first published 1998

Bloomsbury Publishing Plc, 38 Soho Square, London W1V 5DF

Copyright © 1971 Anne Scott-James

The moral right of the author has been asserted

A CIP catalogue record for this book
is available from the British Library

ISBN 0 7475 3697 X

10 9 8 7 6 5 4 3 2 1

Typeset by Hewer Text Composition Services, Edinburgh
Printed in Great Britain by Clays Limited, St Ives plc

To
Osbert

CONTENTS

Acknowlegements

Sincere thanks to the staff of Fison's Ltd. for their help with Chapter V, to Mr P. Stageman of the Lindley Library, for invaluable advice on books, and to Mr Geoffrey Bateman for reading the proofs.

Foreword

That great gardener and nurseryman, Mr Christopher Lloyd, who owns the celebrated show-place, Great Dixter, once wrote that nobody should write about gardening unless he had the nerve to open his own garden to the public. This gave my confidence a terrible shaking. I was writing regular gardening articles at the time for *Queen* magazine, but the idea of opening my garden to the public was laughable.

I own a two-acre cottage garden which is a constant delight to me. As I have had the garden for thirty years, I know every stick and stalk in it and feel that every plant is a personal friend. I remember where I bought this one and who gave me that one, the date when I sowed the seed of these paeonies and the year when I brought those oxlips home in a spongebag from France.

But if I let the public into my garden they would soon be demanding their money back, for it is not a tidy garden. The grass is often ragged, the fences are battered, the old elm trees could do with some trimming and the wild garden is a martyr to stinging nettles. I have never had either the time or money to make it a show garden. I would like a full-time gardener, but I manage with an old man of eighty half a day a week. I would like a paved garden of York stone and a lily pool, but the paving is some sort of synthetic stuff and my lily pool is still in the future.

Yet perhaps my limitations, combined, as they are, with a passionate love of the subject, are themselves a qualification for writing about gardening, for I really do understand the practical problems. This is the way most people garden, always hard pushed for time and cash, the reality never quite catching up with their dreams. Most of us are quite content with the lack of perfection, for there is more pleasure in making a garden than in contemplating a paradise.

The only other virtue I have to offer is that I have seen many of the most beautiful gardens in Britain, particularly the smaller gardens, and I have been lucky enough to spend long days with their owners, asking an infinity of questions and always being given kind and thoughtful answers, for gardeners are not close or stingy, like cooks, who guard the secrets of their recipes. Other gardeners *want* your garden to be good. I have followed up and tested in my own garden many of the ideas I gathered on my tours, and personal suggestions from great gardeners like Mr Harold Hillier and the late Mrs Margery Fish make the penultimate chapter in this book.

I write not as an expert horticulturist but as a working gardener. There are many exciting aspects of the subject which I have not touched, such as greenhouse gardening and water gardening, for the good reason that I know very little about them, and I am skimpy on rhododendrons, which are not a part of general gardening, but a separate world. I have written about my own discoveries, prejudices, setbacks and delights, hoping that the book will help other gardeners who share my problems and my joys.

PART I

In the Mind

CHAPTER I

The Style of Garden

It is a common delusion among gardeners that their art is above the whims of fashion. They know that their taste in clothes changes every year or two; in china, pots and pans, perhaps every ten years; and in decoration, every fifteen or twenty years. But they believe that gardens have an eternal quality and flowers a beauty which does not change, and that they themselves are faithful in their affections to the favourite flowers of their childhood.

This romantic idea is not borne out by the facts. Fashions in gardening change slowly because the elements of a garden are slow to mature, but they move steadily, in step with the social tastes and economic conditions of the time. The grandiose formal gardens of the late 17th century, planned on the mathematical principles of Le Nôtre, were in tune with contemporary society, but they would be objects of derision in modern England. The Victorian garden was essentially right for a prosperous new middle class with servants, money and a passion for mechanical inventions like the lawnmower and for novelties like mass-produced statuary and the hot-water-heated greenhouse – the forcing-ground of all those bedding plants – but it has few disciples now.

Today, too, there is a contemporary style of gardening which is quite different from anything which went before. The gardens of elderly or unsophisticated people, who are naturally reluctant to change, may still show traces of a Victorian or Edwardian manner. But most gardeners, whether consciously or not, are working in a style which is essentially of the 1970's.

The style derives from William Robinson, whose influence is still dominant more than a hundred years after the publication of his first important book. (*The Wild Garden* was published in 1870, *The English Flower Garden* in 1883.) He and his formidable colleague, Gertrude Jekyll, who designed wholly or partly more than three hundred gardens, challenged and vanquished the formal Italianate style which was fashionable with the Victorians and introduced 'natural' gardening, of which the ideal was a total fidelity to nature. Out went carpet bedding, topiary, geometrical layouts, statues and fountains – 'costly rubbish' and 'gigantic watersquirts' as Robinson contemptuously called them, giving a particularly unfavourable mention to Chatsworth. In came naturalized plantings, stream and woodland gardening, herbaceous borders, curved paths and beds, mixtures of exotics with simple native flowers, climbers and creepers, ground cover and a seemingly haphazard beauty.

But gardeners at the turn of the century had plenty of skilled labour. Robinson wrote without a qualm about the need, in the flower garden near the house, for 'the ceaseless care and culture of many and diverse things, often tender and in need of protection, in varied and artificial soils, staking, cleaning, trials of novelties, study of colour effects lasting many weeks, sowings and mowings at all seasons'. And Miss Jekyll's borders required unceasing attention; when the delphiniums had flowered, they would be dead-headed and everlasting peas, planted just behind, would be trained over them to hide the stalks, and when the peas had flowered, *Clematis jackmanii* would be trained over them in turn, and after the *Clematis jackmanii*, a later clematis would be brought forward, so that one group of plants would be worked four times in a season, with trimmings in between. The 'natural' effect was achieved with most unnatural care.

Miss Jekyll thought of her style as a cottage style, but, by our standards, the resources at her disposal were anything but modest.

Few of today's gardeners could attempt this intense cultivation. They may have plenty of money to spend, for gardening is Britain's most popular hobby and many enthusiasts would rather spend money on their gardens than on any other luxury. But skilled hired labour has become almost unobtainable – trained head gardeners are snapped up by municipal authorities and gardener's 'boys' don't exist – and the owner has himself (or more likely, herself) become the working gardener, with perhaps a few hours paid help a week. So Robinson's garden had to develop on labour-saving lines, with shrubs the most important plant material, herbaceous borders cut to a minimum, more hardy and fewer tender plants, less staking, more paving and more permanent planting. A second important change came in the wake of inflation; as the cost of living soared, home-grown vegetables boomed again after years of neglect and today town as well as country gardeners find a corner for fresh produce.

Economics are not the only influence. Our whole manner of living is simpler than when Robinson was letting off his broadsides against Victorian artifice. We eat less, wear less, live in smaller houses and have smaller gardens. Miss Jekyll was accustomed to work on gardens of several acres, where there might be four or five separate herbaceous borders designed in different colour schemes or planned to bloom in different months. Today, 86 per cent of English gardens are smaller than a quarter of an acre, and even in large or medium-sized gardens, the cultivated space is shrinking.

On the other hand, the modern gardener has a fantastic range of new tools and scientific developments to cheer him on his way, from mist propagators to floating motor mowers. Swimming-pools and water gardens are commonplace; new paving materials have encroached on the lawn to make terraces and 'outdoor rooms'; plants which were once tender have been produced in hardier strains and plants which were once rare are produced in quantity.

So it is not all a dead loss, and I am not one of those who mourn for the gardens of yesteryear. I even suspect that we might find Robinson's plantings too heavy for our taste, and some of Miss Jekyll's surviving gardens seem quaint and fussy to modern eyes.

There are perhaps five styles of gardening practised in England today. (I do not count the great 18th-century landscapes which are not true gardens, but pleasure grounds, nor the panoramic gardens of Scotland, Wales and Northern Ireland, where the garden is not so much an adjunct of the house, as part of the scenery.) There are the Suburban Style, the Working-Class Style, the Victorian Style, the Modern Town Style and the greatest of them all, the New Cottage Style, which I consider the true contemporary style and which is the subject of this book.

I would not dream of saying that this style is 'good' and the others are 'bad', for every man is entitled to his own taste, and one man's cherub is another man's gnome. But I consider it the true contemporary style because it is the most English and the most influential, setting the pace in taste and plantsmanship and winning converts all the time. You see it, idealized, in great modern gardens like Sissinghurst. You see it triumphant in thousands of small country houses – the manors, granges, parsonages, cottages, farm-houses and mills with which England is jewelled. And you see it stretching beyond its natural habitat into suburbs and towns. It is very moving the way town gardeners create an atmosphere of deep country in a few square yards of city soil, with clematis clambering over sooty walls and rosemary shrouding the dustbins. Many town and suburban gardeners have changed to the New Cottage Style after visiting some of the beautiful country gardens which are open to the public. They see Sissinghurst or Hidcote or one of the smaller manor houses or rectory gardens, and it is a revelation. When they get home, they think for the first time of planting old-fashioned roses or making a herb garden. Sissinghurst and its gardener-poet, the late V. Sackville-West, have had an immeasurable influence. Spacious and aristocratic though it is, Sissinghurst was largely made under post-war conditions and could be called the first modern garden.

As the New Cottage Style is the subject of this book, I will leave it to the last, taking a bird's-eye view of the other four styles on the way.

The Suburban Garden is the most important numerically, and is the target of most modern gardening books and magazines. The garden is conditioned by its major problem, that of size, for the suburban garden is shrinking fast. A bank manager in Victorian times might have had three acres in Streatham, but today his garden, even if it is on a smart new estate, is probably very small. Usually, the gardener tackles the size problem by making his garden neat and semi-formal. A perfect lawn and hybrid tea roses are key features; others are bedding plants, trellises and pergolas, small trees and shrubs in scale with the garden, fastigiate trees, quick-growing hedges, Darwin tulips, fancy ornaments (gnomes are still buoyant sellers) and pools. In the richer suburban gardens, there is often amazingly expensive garden furniture, from tiled barbecues to chintzy swings. The virtues of the style are neatness and sometimes a high standard of horticultural skill. On the other hand, it is quite without romance, and lacks individuality. It is extremely depressing to see the same ten hybrid tea roses grown in garden after garden in a suburban street.

The Working-Class Garden is on the decline, but survives vigorously in the North of England, where garden fashion has been static for generations. It differs from any other garden by being two-dimensional; with no trees, shrubs or climbers up the house (forbidden by the council or the landlord on many estates), the nearest thing to a vertical line is likely to be a runner bean pole. There is usually no lawn and the most important crops are vegetables and bedding plants. At its best it has vegetables grown to jumbo size – the ideal working-class onion is as big as a football – and neat bedding plants grown like vegetables in rows. At its worst it is a neglected wilderness.

The Victorian Garden – that is, the garden before Robinson and Miss Jekyll got at it – consisting of formal parterres, lawns, gravel walks, laurels, urns, carpet bedding and a monkey puzzle, is now rare. It survives as a pretentious accessory to a few stately mansions, but more often adorns hydropathic hotels and municipal parks. There is a fascinating example at Reading.

The Modern Town Garden makes a virtue of its harsh surroundings, instead of trying to conceal them. The garden is looked on, not as a place for plants, but as an 'outdoor room'. The important elements are architectural, the plants are merely 'infill'. It often has pierced concrete walls, the ground is paved, and it is furnished with plants in tubs, with tables, chairs, and perhaps a children's sandpit or swing, and is understandably popular with parents of young children, for it is almost indestructible.

The New Cottage Style differs fundamentally from the others in being informal. The planning of the garden, whether large or small, allows for change and surprise, so that the whole garden is never seen in one glance, as with the huge formal gardens of Le Nôtre, or the suburban gardens of today. The basis of the planting is mixture.

Plants grow promiscuously, as in nature, clematis intertwining with roses, artichokes and parsley joining choice paeonies in the border. The effect is essentially romantic. Any touch of formality is a conscious conceit.

The garden has many other characteristics besides informality.

It is strongly three-dimensional. There are always important trees, both deciduous and evergreen, and climbing plants in abundance give the garden height.

It is full of slow-growing plants. If the owner has not had the luck to inherit mature trees and slow-growing hedges, he plants them for the future, for there is a quality about slow-growing plants which the instant garden can never match. He waits patiently for hardwood trees which he will never see in maturity and makes hedges of box, holly, beech and yew.

The garden is profusely planted, and for most of the year there is no bare soil to be seen. It is never dug and rarely hoed and mulching takes the place of deep manuring, as in nature. Most of the planting is hardy and permanent.

The most important plants are shrubs – the biggest single change from the Robinson-Jekyll garden – which are planted in rich variety, with rare and choice forms as well as common shrubs. The other essential plant material is ground cover, and the choice of ground cover and foliage plants has lately become an art in itself, with its own literature.

There are masses of roses, particularly shrub roses, old-fashioned roses, rose species, climbing roses, rose hedges and such floribundas as grow gracefully. Scent is more highly prized than size of bloom or brilliance of colour. Hybrid tea roses are usually relegated to the cutting bed.

Colours all over the garden are muted, perhaps even quieter than in Miss Jekyll's gardens, for though she loved grey leaves and foliage plants, she used many showy herbaceous plants, like delphiniums, and was free with a colour which is now right out of fashion – orange. There is also a current whim for green flowers, ferns and grasses. The ultimate in small, green, weedy flowers is the Rose Plantain, an old plant mentioned in Gerard's Herbal, which grows in green whorls and is almost indistinguishable from the plantains which you fight to get out of your lawn. I was given a root of this historic plant a few years ago and cherished it too well, for it seeded all over the garden, and my excuse to visitors that my weeds are in Gerard's Herbal is always greeted with hilarity. I was given by the same kind friend a root of Mr Bowles's Golden Grass, but, alas, somebody weeded it along with the twitch.

The taste for quiet colour is matched by modest ideas about the size of blooms. The giant roses and dahlias which delight specialist gardeners are eyesores to the cottage gardener.

Herbs are important, and are grown in wide variety both in separate herb beds and throughout the garden, a cottage taste which has spread to towns, where herbs have ousted geraniums from many fashionable window-boxes.

Miniature flowers are in fashion, from narcissi to irises. So are plant species, from tulips to roses. So are old-fashioned flowers, like auriculas and the hen-and-chickens daisy. So are traditional cottage mixtures, like sweet williams with lilies. So are alpine plants, so many of which are wild or species forms (alpines are a marvellous field for the collector), more probably grown as paving plants than in a rock garden.

The modern garden is beautiful in winter, which was not the case with older gardens. One of the excuses for the Victorian bedding fashion was that many of the great country houses were used for only one summer month in the whole year, when a stunning display would be needed to impress the family and their guests. Now, we all use our houses hard and want pleasure from the garden all the year round. So the garden is rich in winter-flowering plants and evergreens. Evergreen shrubs are often treated in a consciously historical way, that's to say, formally planted and neatly clipped as they were centuries ago (clipping was anathema to Robinson and Miss Jekyll), and a revival of topiary wouldn't surprise me, if only it weren't so difficult to get your peacock started.

This, then, is the flower garden of the 1970's – informal, three-dimensional, profusely planted, shrubby, herby, permanent, hardy, soft in colour, lively in winter, considerably evergreen, labour-saving, unostentatious. Any snobbery is of the inverted kind.

To any gardener who says 'This is what I've always liked, I haven't changed for twenty years', I would put these questions. 'Did you always like hostas?' 'Did you always have clumps of herbs in the rose-beds?' 'Did you always have a rambler up the apple-tree and a clematis up the plum?' 'Did you always have Hidcote lavender, apple mint, hellebores, species tulips, *Alchemilla mollis, Senecio laxifolius, Rosa rubrifolia, Mahonia japonica, Acer griseum* and the Westonbirt dogwood?'

If he has planted some of these recently for the first time he has sensed a trend and must admit that taste in gardening is not eternal. We, like other generations of gardeners, have our fashionable (and unfashionable) plants.

CHAPTER II

The Bones of a Garden

To me, the most difficult part of gardening is the designing. Few gardeners start with a perfect site, and the days when a landowner could divert a river or shift an inconvenient village are well in the past. Most gardeners have to compromise with their dreams and make something harmonious in the teeth of such little local difficulties as a mound of builder's rubble on the lawn or a pylon in full view of the drawing-room window.

Though a garden is essentially a living thing and will grow and change, so that the design must allow for flexibility, it is yet highly important to get the right bones at the start. Minor changes can and should be made all the time if the garden is not to be a rigid bore, but the basic architecture of the garden and the siting of hardwood trees are expensive, if not impossible, to alter. Where the bones are bad, skilful planting can come to the rescue, but the gardener's task is much more difficult.

My own garden is on a windy slope of the Berkshire downs and has just one sheltered corner protected from both the sharp north winds and the prevailing southwester. This cosy nook is occupied by the dustbins.

This miracle of bad design is almost irremediable and is not entirely my fault. When I bought the cottage in 1938 the house and garden were both very small. The cottage, built in 1806, was like a doll's house and faced west, with a small, steep garden back and front; the south side of the house was only a few feet from the boundary fence, leaving no scope for a south-facing flower bed.

Since then, both the cottage and the garden have grown. Extra rooms have been built on, carved out of the hill, and I was lucky enough to acquire a field at the back surrounded by fine elm trees. Over the years the original back garden hedge has been grubbed up, a tennis court was scooped out of the field, an elm felled to give a vista down the valley, a group of evergreens planted as a windbreak, and a sunk garden made for sitting out (our steep site precludes a terrace next the house); later the tennis court was scrapped, since nobody played on it, leaving a large level lawn with awkward banks in all directions. Another change was enforced by the traffic on our country road which was negligible in 1938, but became fierce by 1960, so that we switched the main centre of cultivation from the front garden to the back. The garden could, to put it mildly, be described as rambling. It was never planned as a whole. It just grew. And there are many gardens like it.

If I could re-make the entire thing from scratch, I would not change it drastically, for I like its oddities. But I could give it a firmer structure. Perhaps a bit more terracing of the slope, and a better pattern of paths, so that each part of the garden led more easily into the next. Not only would I now have the complete site to treat as a unity, but I know much more about garden design than I knew in my salad days. I have spent many hours visiting gardens all over the country, and have seen as many as possible in winter, when the bones are bare and the structure is most clearly revealed.

I don't think anyone can lay down rules for designing gardens in the Cottage Style (formal gardens, like embroidery, can be done by the book), for the style is essentially individual and each gardener must interpret it for himself. But after studying the gardens I love best, from great gardens like Hidcote to small gardens in Chelsea, I have observed that a few basic laws of design are common to many and I have tried to put them together into some sort of code. Every law in the code is breakable, for one can never be dogmatic about gardening, and the unorthodox idea is often the greatest.

Harmony with the Landscape

The most important law in the code is that the garden should harmonize with the landscape. A formal garden can be artificially imposed – there are many unashamedly exotic Italian gardens in England, sublime in the grand manner – but the nature of an informal garden is to blend with the background, the climate and the soil. Nothing is more certainly doomed than a bogus waterfall in a flat country or an azalea garden on chalk downs. Outstanding examples of harmonious design are the chalk garden at Highdown, in Sussex, made in a chalk-pit and filled with chalk-loving plants; of quite an opposite nature, the heather garden at Wisley, a tapestry of heather taking naturally to the acid soil of Surrey; and, quite different again, the lakeside garden at St Columb's, in Co. Donegal, a region of very high rainfall, where simple groups of rain-loving shrubs and bog plants rise out of a meadow of lush Irish grass.

Even this important law of harmony may have to be broken in a town garden. It is no good 'blending with the environment' if the environment is hideous. An ultra-modern gardener, of the concrete-and-infill school, might try to make a 'feature' of a factory chimney, but most gardeners would prefer to mask it with a tree.

A Central Axis

Many of the best informal gardens in England, both large and small, are designed round a long central axis. In the true cottage garden, this usually consists of a central path leading from the gate to the front door, with flowers either side of the path and vegetables behind the flowers.

More sophisticated gardens develop this simple theme so that a central path is still seen from the house in its entirety (probably from the back, not the front), leading to some distant focal point, perhaps a gate, a statue, a seat, a group of shrubs, an arbour or a gap in the skyline; but the ground either side of the path is not open, as in a cottage garden, but concealed from the viewer in the house by walls, hedges, balustrades, espalier trees or other devices, which may be parallel to the path, or at right angles to it. To see the garden, you walk the full length of the path, passing through a series of openings, each leading into a separate garden, until you reach the path's end. The path may change in width and texture – grass may become brick and then stone and then grass again – but the line is continuous.

The finest example of the central axis, passing through a series of gardens and ending in a focal point, is at Hidcote Manor, but the idea is as excellent for a tiny garden as for a large one.

Any writer attempting to describe Hidcote must feel qualms at treading in the footsteps of Miss Sackville-West, and I would urge any gardener who has not already done so to read her poetic essay on this garden, which evokes its spirit as I could never hope to do. But I must squash my diffidence and trace the course of the main axis of the garden, as it is essential to my theme.

Stand with your back to the house and prepare to walk down the central axis which passes through five separate gardens and ends in a wrought-iron gate leading into open country.

You start in the Old Garden, dominated by a fine cedar of Lebanon and enclosed by box hedges clipped into topiary shapes at the corners. Walk down the grass path in the middle of the Old Garden through a gap in the box hedges, down some steps, and into the big Herbaceous Garden, planted chiefly with blue, green, white and mauve flowers. Walk on through an iron gate and you are in the formal Circular Garden. This garden is quite small, just a circle of grass ringed by brick paths and small flower beds, planted with bulbs and hellebores against a background of yew and holly. Walk on through a gap in the hedges and you are in the Red and Purple Garden. The path widens here and has curved edges, and is flanked by deep curved borders of red and purple roses and herbaceous flowers and purple-leaved shrubs and herbs. The borders are backed by dry walling over-topped with yew. Walk on up some stone steps flanked by a pair of Chinese-y summer-houses and you are in the Stilt Garden, where the path, or axis, is flanked by two rows of clipped hornbeams on stems. This is the last garden and it ends in a gate which leads into open parkland.

Many other gardens, both formal and wild, lead off the main axis, and there many other avenues to explore, many hedges to wonder at, many steps to ascend and descend, topiary and water and rare plants to delight in. But the glory of Hidcote is this central axis along which you walk, through gates and gaps, while the garden alternatively expands and contracts beside you. It is to me the climax of garden design. No garden with an open centre can give such variety of experience. I think every gardener who is making a garden, however small, should visit Hidcote before putting a fork into the soil.

Variety of Levels

Of the many design ideas to be seen at Hidcote, three are outstanding: first, the central axis, second, the value of a variety of levels. True, the garden is built on a Cotswold slope, so it couldn't be flat. But the levels have been artificially varied so that you enter and leave nearly every enclosure by steps. I don't mean that it is a toilsome garden of steep flights. But you descend two or three steps into each enclosure, whether square or circular, and ascend as you leave. The eye travels up and down and sees the garden from a variety of angles. The enclosures are mostly of formal shape, but so informally planted that the effect is of 'a cottage garden on the most glorified scale'. (I quote Miss Sackville-West.) There is 'a kind of haphazard luxuriance, which of course comes neither by hap nor hazard at all'. This profusion is to me the essence of gardening.

I know many other gardens of varying sizes and on quite different sites where these two principles have been followed successfully, the principles of the central axis and of variety of levels.

On a grand scale, there is the North Court at Cranborne Manor, in Dorset, a handsome Elizabethan house with a mellow, rambling garden which was first laid out in 1600 by the eldest

John Tradescant. (See the frontispiece.) You look down into the North Court from the North Terrace and see a long path, flanked by espalier fruit trees, passing through the White Garden, then through vast iron gates which open on to a broad avenue of Cornish elms.

On a moderate scale, there is the garden of the Old Rectory, Sulhamstead, Berkshire, one of the loveliest gardens I know, where a long stone path, flanked by mixed borders and over-arched with roses, leads to a sumptuous piece of planting as a focal point: a stone urn surrounded by hostas and lilies inside a semi-circle of cypresses and Irish yews.

On a miniature scale, there is a charming back garden in Cheyne Walk, Chelsea, where steps and a central path provide variety and surprise in a very small space. This garden is only 60 feet long and 24 feet wide. You go out of the back door into a paved garden containing tubs of lilies. Then *up* some steps into the main garden which, like a mini Hidcote, narrows and widens on either side of you as you walk from end to end. You walk first along a grass path flanked by low box hedges with flower-beds behind them planted with cottage flowers; then the path widens into a small central lawn; then it passes under an arch covered with roses; then you go *down* some steps into a paved garden with tiny beds of bedding plants and the focal point of the axis, a garden seat. I feel that any gardener with a flat site should, as in this little garden, either raise or sink part of his garden, for a flat garden is a dull one. Besides, steps are one of the best architectural features in a garden, lending themselves to all manner of plantings.

Separate Rooms

The third principle of Hidcote is that of separate rooms, a most comforting principle for the gardener who has a difficult site, or who has added to his garden, or hasn't the cash for a big landscape project. For a garden of separate enclosures is within every gardener's grasp.

Of course, many gardeners don't want this. Some feel (wrongly,

I think) that an open garden looks larger than it is, while I believe that it looks smaller. The essence of the suburban style is that the centre is open (usually a lawn) and the shape of the garden is seen in a glance. The essence of the New Cottage Style is mystery, and a garden with one enclosure leading to another is nothing if not mysterious. What will the next enclosure contain? Perhaps a herb or water garden, vegetables, a wild garden, a formal Italian garden, or just cool, green grass.

Sissinghurst, like Hidcote, is a garden of many gardens. So is Cranborne Manor. But a garden does not need to be vast to have separate rooms. A garden of an acre or less can be cut by paths and walls into compartments which lead into one another.

The front garden of Mr John Piper's farmhouse in Buckinghamshire covers about an acre, in shape a rectangle, which could be open and dull. But it is cut into quarters by a long central path running down the garden, and by an old brick-and-flint wall running across it, making four rooms. These are planted with a glorious cottage mixture of trees, shrubs, vegetables, fruit, roses, and naturalized plantings of all sorts, and climbers smother both sides of the wall.

Apart from the aesthetic pleasure of separate enclosures this is much the easiest sort of garden to manage. One can so often spare an hour or two for planting or weeding a small space when one could not embark on a large one. And one can re-plan a piece of the garden while keeping the rest in good order.

Nor does this garden rely for effect on a perfectly kept lawn. I have never subscribed to the view that a lawn is labour-saving. I would rather handle flowers or vegetables any day than face the unutterably boring weeding, feeding, cutting, edging and dosing that a lawn requires.

The Siting of Trees

When you have decided on the style of your garden – formal or informal, open or divided – it is time to consider the siting of trees. Few gardens today are made, as was Hidcote, on virgin soil. Most of us have to fit the design to a *status quo*, and though this may mean working with fine trees, mellow walls, a stream or an exquisite prospect, it is more likely to mean shutting out some hideous building, a howling gale or the all too familiar view of a network of posts and wires. Often the answer to such a problem lies in planting trees, the right trees in the right place.

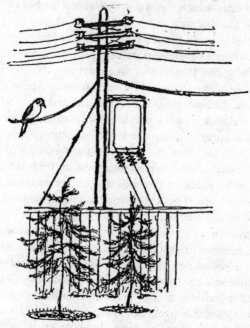

A professional landscape gardener would probably survey the garden and then plan largely on paper, but the owner-gardener will do better with instinct than geometry. In other words, do it by eye, not forgetting the view from the house.

If you want to shut out some eyesore, such as a pylon or an ugly new development, you will need a thick screen which is quick-growing and evergreen, and the most obvious choice is probably the best, *Cupressocyparis leylandii*. Of all the cypresses and thujas, the Leyland cypress is the easiest and fastest, and it is a cheerful, feathery tree, unlike those solid cemetery conifers one associates with showy tombstones and family vaults. If you want the cypresses to grow into mature trees (not a hedge), plant them in a group, not in a row, which always looks institutional.

If you are screening against wind, your trees can, but need not be evergreen. Experts insist that a broken screen is more effective than a solid one, which the wind will go up and over, descending furiously on the far side, and that even a wall is not so good a wind-break as a loose hedge. I find this hard to swallow, for the earliest strawberries and the peachiest peaches always come out of walled gardens, but I must bow to expert knowledge. I admit that thickets of nut-trees have done much to break the wind problem in my own garden, where nuts like the soil and grow to prodigious heights. In a damper soil, I would choose alders or poplars.

If you do choose evergreens for screening, you will want deciduous trees in other parts of the garden, to provide variety of shape and colour, the varieties depending on your acreage.

Anyone with a large garden will want to plant some of the great hardwood trees, for their sheer quality and as a gift to posterity, and some of them grow with surprising speed. A young couple who plant a walnut or a chestnut now will sit in its shade long before middle age. It is essential to think ahead and calculate the ultimate size of your trees accurately, so that you do not find you have an oak-tree pushing its arms through the drawing-room window.

In a smaller garden, it is even more important to choose trees in proportion, and it is pathetic how often one sees a small garden smothered by too ambitious a tree, perhaps the lovely but large Tree of Heaven, more usually the giant weeping willow, *Salix alba* 'Tristis'. The weeping willows by the bridge at Sonning, on the Thames, sweeping the river with their trembling branches, are one thing. A weeping willow in the small, dry garden of a modern villa is quite another. The French, whose taste in small gardens is deplorable (their *forte* is forestry), have gone quite mad for weeping willows, and there is scarcely a villa in *la belle France* without one, its pale green shoots clashing noisomely with new pink brick, its drooping shape a silly cliché in the naked square which serves the average Frenchman for a garden.

There are many small trees which would be better than the willow as the one main tree in a small garden, or as a group in a garden of an acre or two. The whitebeam is a soft, silvery tree, especially the variety *Sorbus aria* 'Lutescens'. There are many varieties of crataegus which have good shape, good berries and a good constitution – *C. prunifolia* is one of the finest, with crimson leaves in autumn and huge berries. The Willow Leaf Pear, *Pyrus salicifolia* 'Pendula', is a charming and most manageable tree. The aralias grow to a useful 30 feet, as do some of the robinias. The list of ornamental cherries is long and honourable – I like the

white-flowered ones best myself, for most of the pink ones insist
on coming out with the daffodils. If you want a highly unusual
small tree, which is nonetheless not difficult to grow, you might like
the decorative, candelabra-branched dogwood, *Cornus controversa*
'Variegata'. Or perhaps the Judas-tree, *Cercis siliquastrum*, with
clusters of purple-pink pea-flowers in May.

Then there are many small weeping trees and fastigiate trees, both
ideal for a small garden, in their different ways. An evening spent
with a good catalogue, like Hillier's or Sherrard's, will reveal an
astonishingly wide range of both weepers and fastigiates. Whatever
sort of tree the gardener has in his mind's eye, whether large or small,
for screening or for ornament, he would do well to read *Collins
Guide to Tree Planting and Cultivation*, by H. L. Edlin, before
making his final choice; this new, excellent book is an insurance
against mistakes and disappointments.

Picture Gardeners Versus Plantsmen

When you have decided on your style, and sited your trees, you can
think about the disposition of flower-beds, grass, shrubs and what
I call 'hardware', meaning steps, terraces, paths or internal walls
which are to be of brick, stone or synthetic stone. This chapter is
about design, not planting, but the two are interwoven, and you
must decide at a fairly early stage how far you want to group
your plants.

The choice, here, is a matter of temperament. No book can help.
It depends on how you think of your garden, and on whether you
are, by nature, a picture-gardener or a plantsman. There have been
great gardeners of both schools.

The classic example of a picture-gardener was Miss Jekyll, who
thought in terms of garden pictures to be seen from the house and
from points of vantage in the garden. She grouped her plants, like
an artist, to get vistas and perspectives, massed colour effects and
beautiful forms. Spotty planting, wrote Miss Jekyll, was 'like a
library of odd single volumes where there should be complete
sets'. To get a garden picture, a theme must be repeated, which

means selecting and eliminating, and there is bound to be some loss of variety. It takes not only an artistic eye but strength of mind.

The paragon of a plantsman was Mr E. A. Bowles, who was a great botanist as well as a gardener, and had a passion for collecting many forms of plants and for cultivating rarities. 'I fear I am little impatient,' wrote Mr Bowles, 'of the school of gardening that encourages the selection of plants merely as artistic furniture, chosen for colour only, like ribbons or embroidery silks.' (I presume he was getting at Miss Jekyll.) And in my own time, and how lucky I was to know her, there was Mrs Margery Fish, who grew no fewer than seven different forms of the lesser periwinkle and thought it boring, when you had one good form of a plant, to choose the same form again. Her garden was to some eyes a treasure-house of plants and to others a 'floral chaos' – Miss Jekyll would certainly have deplored it. I myself was enchanted with it and am somewhat on the plantsman's side of the fence, partly because I love collecting but partly sour grapes – even when I try to group things, my planting seems to come out spotty.

Whether you're a picture-gardener or a plantsman, there are certain principles to consider when you come to the disposition of your beds and other garden features.

Utility Buildings and Hardware

Decide at an early stage where to site your utility buildings. A good shed, a greenhouse or a frame, if you want one, a compost bin and a bonfire must all go somewhere and you will find it difficult to fit them conveniently into a finished design. At the same stage, plan your water supply, with taps at strategic places.

Plan at the same time for a good proportion of hardware – more in a country garden than in a town or village garden, where there are buildings all round. A town garden needs as much green as possible. A country garden needs hardware to contrast with trees and fields. If, in a one-or-two-acre country garden, you can provide a terrace outside the house, some steps flanked by small shrubs or rock plants, at least one hard path with plants spilling or creeping over it, at least one bed raised by a wall so that the drainage is good for lilies and herbs, you are on the way to getting a good proportion of hardware. A terrace is an inestimable blessing, and it is worth trying to plan it so that you can wheel a trolley straight on to it from the house. A hard path all round the garden is also a comfort in bad weather, especially if you have a kitchen garden and have to slosh through the rain to pick your lunch.

Sun, Shade and Wind

While you are thinking about the hardware, you must also consider your aspects. If you can provide a wall, fence or hedge facing south, make an important bed there, don't waste it on grass. (If it's a hedge, leave a path between hedge and bed, or the hedge will take all the best food.) I find I never have enough walls and fences, as I have a passion for climbing plants and frequently find myself nursing a clematis or rose which I can't place. Get in as many walls and fences as you reasonably can, and if you are building new ones, see that nails or vine eyes are built into them at the time of construction to hold climbing plants later. I have never yet known a builder who suggested this to his client, but it ought to be automatic.

Before you plan your sitting-out place, observe the position of sun and shade in various parts of the garden at various times of day. And plan protection from the worst wind, which is not the same in every garden.

In my own garden, the south-wester is much worse than the north or east wind, for it is funnelled up a valley and arrives in furious force. I have had to plant shelter shrubs on the south which shut out a certain amount of sun, but as there are plenty of plants which enjoy shade, I think the loss of light a lesser evil than the blasts of the south-west gale.

When planting hedges, look ahead and choose the varieties of hedge which will last a life-time. Instant hedges of privet or lonicera soon go ragged, but yew, beech, box, hornbeam and holly, once established, become almost architecture and need only one or two clippings a year. For inspiration on the art of hedge-planting pay a visit to Hidcote, which has the finest hedges in the world.

Easy Flower-Beds

Make your flower-beds easy of access. Here, the layout of the great gardens is no help to the owner-gardener. Gardens planned in the days of skilled labour often have beds up to 20 feet deep, backed by walls. In such deep beds, the plants are difficult to get at, and, to avoid packing the soil when they tread on it, the gardeners often have to resort to the tedious device of working from a plank.

In the best smaller gardens I know, the borders are usually no more than 8 feet wide, and always have access from either side. Whether the border is backed by a hedge, a fence or a wall, a 2-foot path is left between. Where the borders are deeper than 8 feet, the gardener can make access easier with the device of stepping-stones at strategic places.

Another means to easy working is an island bed, where shrubs and ground cover readily look natural and at home. I am not so happy about herbaceous plants in island beds; the tradition of herbaceous borders designed to be viewed lengthwise is very strong, and I can't readily accept delphiniums sticking up in the middle of a floating kidney bed.

Of course, when an owner-gardener, rather than a professional landscape gardener, is making a garden, his creative planning will not be done in any rigid order, nor all at once. It is obviously sensible to get construction work and tree planting done at the beginning, but after that the design and the plants will grow together, and the plan will develop in unexpected ways. No gardener need ever be afraid to change his plans, for almost all plants, except yew, ilex and holly, can be moved, even in middle age, in nice wet weather. I have known whole gardens to be moved, including mature trees and shrubs, with scarcely a loss among thousands of plants.

The best gardens are harmonious and serene, but not too obviously planned nor over-finished. Gardens like to go their own way.

CHAPTER III

Stocking the Garden

When making a new garden, or reclaiming a wilderness, most of us have to start with a bulk order from a nursery. But even if these plants are bumper specimens and thrive from the start, it is years before they inspire deep affection, because they came in a batch, like a box of groceries. I find that the plants I love most were all acquired in a more personal way. They were given me by friends, or I collected them wild, or I propagated them, amateurishly, myself.

The plants one is given become part of one's life. I remember who gave me each one, and the occasion, and what the weather was like, and who was of the party. I am almost the only literate person in England who is not planning to write an autobiography, but if I were ever to change my mind, my garden would be a better memory-jogger than my diary, which is crammed with inglorious entries like '10.30, hairdresser' and 'see tax inspector at 2.0'.

Anyone who has been gardening for a year or two will have gardening friends, and gifts of seeds, roots and cuttings soon start to pour in. I myself have been lucky enough to visit gardens as a professional writer, and the loot I have acquired is formidable.

One of the first gardens I wrote about was Mrs Fish's at East Lambrook Manor, and not only was Mrs Fish the most generous of gardeners, but her garden was so thickly planted that when she dug up a plant for you, stray roots of surrounding plants came up with it, and you got a sort of lucky dip. I used to nurture these bits and pieces and they always grew. Some of these stray hairs grew into a colony of pink astrantias and others into a clump of white species phlox; and there was the old-fashioned pansy, Irish Mollie, which Mrs Fish called Dirty Mollie, because it has a brown-and-yellow face in need of a wash; and the satiny *Campanula* 'Burghaltii'; and various herbs which I haven't yet identified.

Every time I go round the garden with my husband, which can be several times a day, we discuss the origins and careers of our plants, sometimes harmoniously but often with acrimony. Unpleasant laughter is aroused by the charming clump of *Veronica gentianoides* 'Variegata' which Mrs Ralph Merton, a dedicated garderner who had just been to Japan and the Antipodes, gave my husband together with a rare lily from New Zealand. My husband got the descriptions mixed and told everybody it was a rare hosta from Fujiyama. Although it never looked remotely like a hosta, one felt that anything could come from Fujiyama, and all were deceived until Mr Eliott Hodgkin came to lunch, a collector of rare plants and a member of the R.H.S. Council, who said, to our humiliation, 'I like your veronica'. My husband took against it from that moment, but I am very fond of the plant.

Then there's the decorative elder which Mr Derek Hill gave us when we went to stay with him in Ireland, where he painted my husband's portrait. His garden is damp and peaty and ours is dry and chalky, but some of the nicest plants are universal. There's the *Genista lydia* brought as booty from a visit to Mr Will Ingwersen's nursery, in the course of which he kindly took me round William Robinson's old garden at Gravetye nearby, showing me which are the original Robinson plantings and which are of later vintage. And the violets which Miss Valerie Finnis gave me at Waterperry, and the clematis we bought from the plant stall at Sissinghurst. There are the hellebores of which Mr H. E. Bates sent me seeds after reading a garden piece I had written in the *Daily Mail*, with instructions for growing them by stratification, and our clumps of *H. corsicus* are now known to us as 'Old Stratification' or 'Old H.

E. Bates'. And the heracleums which Mr John Piper, a great man for thistles and umbels, gave us as seedlings. And the catmint given us by our neighbour, the editor of *Private Eye*. And there are the many enormous plants, quite out of scale with my garden, which my husband brought from his former large garden at Henley, a permanent source of interest and discord. I appreciate that the huge tree paeonies which have done in many of my herbaceous plants have to be kept for reasons of piety, but *must* we have the giant *Viburnum fragrans* which once grew against a wall and which now, in an open bed, is a distorted object with three round sides and one flat one?

When given presents of unusual plants, it is important to try to get the right identification at the time, for it will be much more difficult later. And when you get plants home, plant them at once, however tired you are, and water them copiously. If you do this, you can move plants at almost any season, even in full flower. It's wise to grab every offer when it's made.

The pleasure of giving plants away is as great as that of cashing in, and one follows their fortunes in after-life like a schoolmistress keeping in touch with old pupils. 'And how is our tansy doing? Smothered everything else in the garden? Oh, I'm sorry about that.' 'How's the galega? Completely vanished? I must give you some more.' The best advice I can give to anyone wishing to increase and share his garden stock is 'Get yourself some gardening friends'.

Another way of stocking up with personal plants is to collect them wild, and here I shall be accused of vandalism by the Wild Life people, whom I respect.

I was brought up by high-minded parents to believe that to dig up a wild plant, or even to take its seeds, was a crime, and I never committed it until about five years ago. Then I went back to a spot where I used to look for marsh violets every spring to find it built over with bungalows; and at about the same time I found that some hedgerows where Ragged Robin used to grow have Ragged Robin no more, and that the wild succory of our downland verges is disappearing fast, from the ravages of cutting machinery or possibly herbicides; while a favourite wood in Sussex, once filled with fox-gloves and orchids, including the uncommon butterfly orchid, has been sprayed by The Forestry Commission, no less, to kill the undergrowth. As a result, I have changed my tune. I feel that wild flowers might as well be preserved in my garden as be left to their fate, and I do sometimes dig up a plant, always on a wet day, choosing a large plant, dividing it and replanting half. I have done this locally with hellebores, cowslips and primroses, but not with *Anemone pulsatilla*, for the downland where it grows is reasonably safe from development and the plant is rare. Careful as I am, the practice may still be wrong, but I am not propounding a moral theory, just telling truthfully what I do.

It is curious that a wild plant brought into the garden often requires cushier treatment than it gets in nature. Our local wild hellebores grow in deep shade, but I find that in the garden they prefer a bit of sun; and the cowslips by no means enjoy the dry, tight turf of the downs when they arrive in the garden, but prefer rich soil and mulches of leaf-mould. However, the standard of living of foreign, especially Mediterranean, plants should not be raised too fast, or they may die of spoiling.

Plants collected abroad have even stronger associations for the gardener than native plants, and if collected on a holiday which was (or seems in retrospect) idyllic, they become charged with sentiment. It's illogical, but I find that people who have conscientious objections to plant collecting at home seem to think it quite respectable on foreign soil.

If you want to import wild plants into Britain, there are regulations to be observed, but they are simple. You apply to the Plant Health Branch of the Ministry of Agriculture for a Wild Plant Licence, stating when and where you are going and giving some sort of credentials, such as membership of the R.H.S., and I believe a licence is nearly always granted. A list of forbidden plants is sent with the licence, but these are mostly trees.

Your collecting equipment will be a fern trowel and some plastic bags for seeds, plants and cuttings. Put seeds in moist moss or sand, plants and cuttings in wet moss or peat. In most countries, a spring holiday is more rewarding than a summer one. In Greece, for instance, so thick with flowers in spring, there is scarcely a green blade to be seen after the end of June, only the hot bulbs and stiff stalks of asphodel. Even in Corsica, in early August, most of the seeds of the maquis are already shed.

In France, it is heartening to see how profusely wild flowers still grow in spring. Every road is sashed with violets and cowslips, every copse and bank is tapestried with primroses, hellebores, orchids, cuckoo-flowers, oxlips, euphorbias and pink-and-blue pulmonaria. I suppose the profusion is a sign of a backward agriculture, and that soon the French meadows will be scythed and sprayed like our own. Meanwhile, they are still full of flowers seeding where they will, and, rightly or wrongly, I and many others who love wild plants in the garden sometimes bring a few of the common varieties (never the rare ones) home.

A third way of increasing and improving your basic stock is by propagation, and the further back you go in the creative process, the closer your relationship with the plant. A slow-growing plant, like a tree paeony, grown from seed, fills you with parental pride when, perhaps six years after sowing, it bursts into flower. To me, the best tree in my garden is a large productive walnut, grown, with no skill at all, from a nut left over from lunch.

I have not nearly as many home-propagated plants as I would like because it is only recently that my life has become sufficiently stationary for me to consider a greenhouse. Formerly, I had to leave my garden frequently and plants had to take their chance. But without a greenhouse, or even a frame, one can propagate many plants outdoors.

The ABC of propagation is, of course, the division of herbaceous plants and the sowing of hardy seeds in open ground, but one can go well beyond that.

Many deciduous shrubs and woody plants can be propagated outdoors by hardwood cuttings in a sandy mixture in a pot or well-drained bed out of strong sunlight. Shrubs like forsythia, deutzia and philadelphus are easy, and woody herbs like lavender and sage. Softwood cuttings of geraniums and pinks are easy. The side shoots of *Euphorbia wulfenii* will strike out-of-doors in a pot of sandy soil covered with a plastic bag. Clematis can be propagated by layering into a pot, winter jasmine can be layered into the open ground. Shrubs like *Hypericum patulum* can have the outer shoots removed together with their roots and transplanted. Seeds with a hard outer covering, like holly, tree paeonies and hellebores, can be persuaded to germinate by stratification (see page 158).

Much of this is rough-and-ready work, and a gardener with a greenhouse would get more consistent results than I do in the open. But the gardener who travels frequently or has other things to do can still enjoy a bit of nursery work.

Just as welcome as the plants one has intentionally propagated are the plants which seed themselves. The one reward for doing all one's own weeding is that among the groundsel and the bindweed there is so often a treasure which nobody but the owner-gardener would recognize. At the end of a hellish morning with the thistles, to find a perfect little self-sown *Mahonia japonica* is a pleasure which sends one rushing into the house to shout the joyful news and call for a gin-and-tonic. A shrub seedling is always more exciting than seedlings of bulbs, annuals or herbaceous plants, many of which seed only too easily and can become a nuisance.

I am not suggesting for a moment that one can, or should, do without plants from commercial nurseries. I go to most of the R.H.S. fortnightly shows and usually place one or two modest orders, especially for shrubs and bulbs. At these small, uncrowded shows it is easier to consult the growers than it is in the scrum of Chelsea, where friends in garden-party hats are apt to tap one on the shoulder just as one has caught the attention of the herb man and is concentrating on bronze fennel. And of course I buy from catalogues, which I find the ideal bedside reading. If you are baffled by a long, unfamiliar list of varieties, give special attention to those marked A.G.M., which is the R.H.S. Award of Garden Merit, a good signpost to plants of quality.

I also buy quite a few plants at garden centres, which I enjoy and think are much maligned. A garden centre is necessarily a 'pop' way of buying, and I doubt if the true connoisseur would stoop to it. It cannot stock rarities, though a large centre may stock as many as

3,000 plant varieties in a year – nursery plants in the winter and container-grown plants in the summer. One hears complaints that plants sold in containers are not genuinely container-grown, but have been pushed into their pots at the last minute, but, going only to reputable centres, I have never had this experience. On the contrary, I have sometimes found that the plants have been *too long* in the container and become pot-bound, but a good centre will put such plants on the 'remnants' table.

Container-grown plants are as useful to a busy gardener as Marks and Spencer to a housewife. You buy and plant them when it suits you, there is no root disturbance to the plant and no heeling in while you wait for better weather, and the plants are splendid for filling gaps. There are a few things one should know about garden centre buying. Don't buy nursery stock at the tail end of the winter, when the best stuff will have gone, nor container-grown things too early in the summer – wait until the container-grown season is in full swing. When planting, throw away the container, even if it is the sort which is supposed to rot in the ground, and water lavishly until the plant is established.

When I bought my first container-grown plant, I felt a sense of guilt, born of Puritan inhibitions, about reaping what I had not sowed. Now I tuck pot-grown Irish yews into the boot of the car without a qualm. Instant gardening is no substitute for growing things from the basic pip, but it's a great aid to busy people.

I'm afraid that I enjoy the process of collecting plants so much that my garden will always be a bit of a muddle. I cannot bring myself to put favourite plants on the scrap-heap, even in senility, and I love too many different varieties for the garden to be rich in 'garden pictures'. But if my garden lacks instant impact on the visitor, it is passionately interesting to ourselves.

PART II

On the Ground

CHAPTER IV

Planting for Profusion

On the first day in June, every photographer in England who knows a lupin from a dandelion loads his cameras, gets into his car, and beetles off to photograph gardens. For the rich, prodigal look which most of us want in the garden is at its most luscious and poetic during the first flush of roses. If you can't get a profusion of flowers in June, when the Albertine is waving round the chimney tops, Madame Alfred Carrière is wreathed round the apple trees and the rugosa hedge is bursting into scented blossom, you might as well give up gardening altogether. Nastily, I sometimes wonder if the rose-smothered gardens which make our mouths water in the gardening books and magazines look equally sumptuous in April or August. I know at least one celebrated garden which is superb in June, but heavy and spent by mid-July. It is a one-flower garden, relying too much on roses.

True profusion is more lasting. A garden can look luxuriant for at least eight months a year if one acknowledges that many things are needed besides roses. The gardener must resist the seduction of rose catalogues, and not buy roses to the exclusion of everything else. I admit that their romantic names lead me astray every year, and I have only got to see the words Honorine de Brabant, Fantin-Latour or La Reine Victoria to start filling up the order form.

The surest way of achieving the profuse look which most of us long for would be to up sticks and move to a district with a fertile soil and high rainfall. (In the peaty gardens of the West of Ireland, plants swirl out of the soil and drip from trees as in the Brazilian jungle.) But most of us garden where we happen to be and there is scarcely a garden, even on the dry East Coast or the windy South Downs, which cannot be made luxuriant with good planting and feeding. If you look at a luxuriant garden, and try to analyse its make-up, you will usually find six elements: thick planting; a high proportion of climbing plants; colonies of naturalized plants, especially bulbs; a skilful choice of plants with a long flowering season, or a repeat flowering, especially important with roses; a generous use of foliage plants, ground cover plants and edging plants; and plenty of trailing and creeping plants. Even in a small garden, all these methods of planting, if the gardener wishes, can be used together.

Thick Planting

The most important thing is to clothe the garden with thick planting. One must be brave and ignore the statutory rules about distance between plants – they are traditional head gardener's rules and date back to bedding days – and plant more closely, feeding the soil well so that it can support a dense population.

Nearly all the gardeners I admire most have told me that plants are *happy* in close company, and they put two or three plants in a space where a timid gardener would only put one. H. E. Bates, a novelist, like D. H. Lawrence, whose love of nature permeates his writing, and whose cottage garden in Kent is crammed with flowers, told me 'Put 'em in thick, they are happy in company', and the great Mrs Fish said the same thing: 'Plants are happy in close company, plant much more thickly than they tell you in the books'. And don't only plant closely, but choose plants with a rich manner of growth.

Some plants have a generous shape and others have a meagre shape, and though the skimpy ones may have other merits (often they provide the best flowers for cutting) the most prodigal gardens I know are stuffed with shrubs which billow or spray, with herbaceous plants which grow into fat cushions, and with plants with large, showy leaves.

Outstanding shrubs for clothing a garden are the dogwoods, the viburnums, camellias, hydrangeas, rhododendrons, some of the cotoneasters, especially the weeping and prostrate forms; weigela and its cousin *Kolkwitzia amabilis*; the wonderful elaeagnus tribe; skimmia, *Phlomis fruticosa*, many of the berberis, most of the mahonias, deutzia, escallonia and the shrubby spiraeas, senecios and hypericums. (I will suggest varieties later.)

Outstanding cushion plants are the hardy geraniums, astrantia, astilbe, rue, lavender, nepeta, the heathers, all the shrubby potentillas, *Iberis sempervirens*, many euphorbias, hellebores, *Alchemilla mollis*, pinks (I can't praise them too highly), apple mint, Japanese anemones, santolina, cistus, the thymes and sages and the sedums.

Plants with showy leaves give great value, for leaves usually stay in their prime much longer than flowers. I have relegated the smaller foliage plants to the section on Ground Cover later in this chapter. Of the larger foliage plants, some of the best are the hellebores, with their handsome, deep-cut leaves which never take a day off; *Euphorbia wulfenii*; rodgersia, with large chestnut-shaped leaves; *Alchemilla mollis*, so graceful in its flowers, leaves and manner of growth that it has to be praised in every category; *Acanthus spinosus*, if you have masses of space, for its classical leaves are evocative and exciting, but killers in a small bed; the lofty 8-foot tall macleaya or bocconia, with huge grey-green leaves fingered and veined like a human hand; and royal fern and gunnera if your garden has a stream or pool. Many gardeners would add the larger tree paeonies, especially *P. lutea ludlowii*, but as will appear later, I have a prejudice against this plant, for it hogs space and is a greedy feeder.

Most writers are delighted to praise plants, but are reluctant to criticize, but this is craven. Some plants have really dreary shapes and one should know it, and plant them, if one likes the flowers, where their scrawny outlines will be hidden.

Forsythia is a shrub with no shape at all: *Hibiscus syriacus* has a dreary structure; I wouldn't pack a garden with lilacs, lovely as they are in May, for they are deadly when not in flower; Michaelmas daisies are vitality sappers; and one must admit that hybrid tea and floribunda roses are shapeless collections of sticks and thorns when not in bloom.

Shrubs and Cushion Plants: Some Varieties

Only a specialist of the highest class – the sort of man who writes a monograph – could hope to know all the varieties of even one family of good clothing plants. Some of the great plant families have hundreds, even thousands, of members. The rest of us must see as many as we can in gardens and arboreta and then keep our noses in the catalogues until we find what we want. I won't attempt lengthy lists but will pinpoint a few varieties for whose performance I can vouch, having either grown them myself or followed their progress in the gardens of my friends. I won't try to name camellias or rhododendrons, because I cannot touch them on my chalky soil.

Of the many good dogwoods, I think the loveliest are those with variegated leaves. *Cornus alba* 'Elegantissima' has pale green leaves margined with creamy white and looks its best against a dark background, perhaps a yew or holly hedge, or a tall Irish yew. Some gardeners prefer the Westonbirt dogwood, which has more brilliantly red stems in winter, but in summer its leaves are plain green and not so pretty, and I prefer 'Elegantissima' myself. *C. a.* 'Spaethii' is another good dogwood, with golden-variegated leaves which stay fresh all summer through, and W. J. Bean considered it the finest of all deciduous yellow-variegated shrubs. *C. kousa* is an unusual shrub of considerable size which is covered with delicate white bracts, like a cloud of butterflies, in June.

Of the viburnums, every gardener has his favourite, and mine is *V. tomentosum* 'Mariesii', which has white panicles of lace-cap flowers on flat, candelabra branches. It looks best as a solitary shrub, where it can be admired from every side, for it has a miraculous manner of growth, branching first to one side and then to another, so that it seems to sway like a lady manipulating a crinoline.

The cotoneasters are an enormous and splendid shrub family of which I with difficulty pick three. C. 'Rothschildianus' is something rather special, a large, spreading evergreen shrub with bunches of yellow fruit in autumn and winter; C. *watereri* is a useful tall shrub or small tree growing up to 20 feet or more, semi-evergreen, with masses of red berries which, unlike holly berries, do not seem to get stripped by thievish birds. In the hard December of 1969, the birds ate all my holly berries the week before Christmas, and I was driven to using a sprig of C. *watereri* in the Christmas pudding. Of the numerous prostrate cotoneasters, I suggest C. *salicifolius* 'Autumn Fire', which spreads gracefully and has large sensational clusters of scarlet fruit.

Of the elaeagnus family, I would not be without E. *pungens* 'Maculata', a slow but bushy grower, or E. *ebbingei*, both of which I have described in another chapter (The Garden In Winter).

I wouldn't look at any weigela except the variegated one, W. *florida* 'Variegata', and I think all the best shrubby spiraeas are white, especially S. *arguta*, the 'Bridal Wreath', and S. *thunbergii*. Don't touch the pink-flowered shrubby spiraeas, which look incurably common.

Of the cushion plants, the earliest to flower in my own garden is *Euphorbia epithymoides*, with sulphur yellow flowers and leaves which grow into increasingly large clumps all summer through, and need to be cut back when they grow too heavy. Of the hardy geraniums, G. *psilostemon* is the most exciting, its magenta flowers splashed with a dark eye, but perhaps it is rather tall to be called a cushion. G. *endressii* is a better filler, for it flowers for at least three months, and, if the cushion gets straggly, clip it and it plumps up again. The most interesting astrantia, if you can get it, has variegated leaves (it is currently on the Sunningdale Nurseries list).

Of the shrubby potentillas, P. *fruticosa* 'Elizabeth' has the largest flowers, of bright yellow, but there are many good potentillas and they are well stocked by garden centres, so you can choose for yourself on the spot. Of the hellebores, *H. corsicus* is the most spectacular, but all the hellebores I know have good clumpy shape and beautiful leaves except *H. niger*, which is a disaster in my garden, so often the victim of slugs, rain and general rot that I have given it up.

Of the cistuses, *C. purpureus* is by far the prettiest, growing into three-foot mounds if you are clever enough to get it through three winters without frost damage. Its flowers are of tissue-paper texture, orchid pink with a purple eye. But I find the hardiest in my garden is *C. corbariensis*, with dark glossy leaves and white flowers with a yellow eye. It has survived two really bad winters when other cistuses have succumbed.

The most often praised sedum is *S. spectabile* 'Autumn Joy' and it is certainly the strongest grower, with huge clusters of tawny-red flowers, but I prefer *S. s. atropurpureum*. It is smaller and does not need staking, which 'Autumn Joy' often requires, and the colour is a softer and subtler pink. If there's room, one should grow both.

Of the thymes, I can't speak too highly of lemon thyme, *Thymus citriodorus*, a denser plant than the common thyme, with greener leaves, and brighter pink flowers, very robust and hardy in a dry, well-drained position.

Climbing Plants

Climbing plants are essentially luxuriant because they give so much leaf and flower in proportion to their ground space. They are a gift for the small garden and the town garden. They romanticize everything they touch, and the scramblings and ramblings of a few dozen climbers can give the drabbest villa on a by-pass the aura of a moated grange. Their wanderings are mysterious and unpredictable, for however carefully you train a climber, it will always have a will of its own. Pin up a clematis one evening, and by the morning, stray tendrils will have crept into new positions, showing you clearly that the plant means to plan its own journey.

A few years ago I happened to see two gardens in the same week which were particularly thickly planted with climbers. The gardens were utterly different in size and situation – one a large country garden, the other a small town one – but both were models of the use of the third dimension to swell the produce. The first was at Charleston Manor, in Sussex, where Lady Birley, widow of the painter, Sir Oswald Birley, has made a highly romantic garden in a bowl of the chalk downs.

Charleston Manor is partly Norman, partly Elizabethan, but mostly Queen Anne, and every inch of the house itself, and its barns, dove-cote and outbuildings, is covered with climbers – roses, honey-suckles, clematis, jasmine, wisteria, chaenomeles, ivies, vines, and the lovely climbing hydrangea, *H. petiolaris*.

All over the garden, which has lawns, yew walks, orchards and a little piece of woodland, there are more climbers, growing up trees, or up host plants, or up tripods made of wood stakes, or up obelisks of wire mesh. Everything that can support a climber is used except pergolas and trellis. Nearly always, two or three climbers are planted together: an orange Magic Carpet rose is paired with yellow Wedding Day; creamy-white Madame Alfred Carrière with blush-pink Madame Butterfly; deep red Etoile de Hollande with white, semi-double Bobbie James; a flesh-pink Adelaide d'Orléans rose goes with late-flowering *Clematis orientalis*.

To prolong the flowering season, a late climber is often grown up an earlier climber, such as a summer clematis up a spring-flowering wisteria. The apple orchard has three climbers planted at the foot of every tree, so that when the fruit blossom is over, the roses and clematis begin, and, as their flowers die, the apples start fruiting. Charleston Manor is on chalk, without much topsoil, and, since every square of ground has to yield so much, the garden needs – and gets – rich feeding.

The garden of Charleston Manor is a large one. The other garden I saw that week is no more than a patch. It belongs to a house in Kensington with a front and a back garden each 25 feet by 35 feet in size. Both are crowded with shrubs, some familiar and some rare, with herbs, euphorbias, hellebores, hostas, camellias, succulents, rock plants, rue and bay, all planted with an artist's feeling for colour and form, and the eye is carried up to the sky by no fewer than forty clematis. The thick, rich planting of these two pocket handkerchiefs of soil, with two or three plants growing out of a space where the less accomplished gardener would put but one, makes it a garden of the highest quality, an encouragement to every gardener who feels imprisoned by the smallness of his ground.

In my own garden, I am pathetically short of wall space, because most of my boundaries are old thick hedges and I haven't an infinite supply of the old apple trees which Miss Sackville-West innocently assumed to be part of the furniture of every garden. But I have found corners somehow for clematis, honeysuckle, a vine, climbing roses and *Hydrangea petiolaris*. I have clematis at most seasons, starting with C. *macropetala*, then C. *montana*, then 'Nelly Moser', then C. 'Alba Luxurians', which has unusual white flowers tipped with green and finally the yellow-lantern clematis, C. *orientalis*, which is a joy in late summer (I believe C. *tangutica* is even better).

Of the climbing roses, my favourite is New Dawn, surely one of the best climbers ever bred, with small glossy leaves and a succession of scented shell-pink flowers which do not turn an ugly brown and cling on, like the flowers of Albertine; New Dawn just lets her faded petals fall politely to the ground. Of the red climbers, my first love was Etoile de Hollande, but mine is not as prolific as she was and I am trying Guinée, *almost* as dark a red and *almost* as strongly scented, as a successor. I think the best yellow climber is Mermaid, but my cottage isn't high enough for this gigantic grower.

Naturalization

Another means to profusion – by naturalization – is not for the very small garden, though a quarter of an acre might well have one or two naturalized plantings.

Naturalizing means planting things where they will take care of themselves. Bulbs left to multiply in grass or woodland, primroses left to increase in a bank or yellow loosestrife in a dell, or some hardy annual, like sweet rocket or nigella, left to seed itself, are all naturalized. The gardener does little more than keep the plants clear of rank weeds which might smother them.

The beauty of such plantings is their free and wild look. No gardener could ever plant snowdrops or daffodils with the grace with which they group themselves, and I don't think lilies in beds ever have quite the perfection of lilies in a wood. They have a spontaneity which can't be copied.

But they can also be dreadfully untidy, especially when dying down, which is why naturalizing is difficult in a small garden. Grass in which daffodils are naturalized cannot be mown until mid-June, which is something of a sacrifice for the gardener who loves a smooth lawn and hasn't room for a meadow as well. But even in a small garden, a little space should be squeezed for naturalizing if you want an air of profusion. One idea is to stuff masses of very early bulbs in the lawn, which will have died down by the time you want to mow. Sometimes space can be found under a tree for naturalizing groups of daffodils, martagon lilies, primroses, hellebores, or *Cyclamen neapolitanum*.

In a larger garden, the choice of suitable plants is very wide and unexpected plants, like paeonies and species roses, naturalize perfectly. I have gone more fully into the subject of wild gardening in Chapter VI.

I have left two other ways to profusion, also, for other chapters: for ideas on plants with a long flowering season, or a repeat season, turn to Chapter IX on *Roses* and to Chapter VIII on *Ruth Draper Time*.

Foliage Plants and Ground Cover

Foliage plants and ground cover plants have, like shrubs, emerged from obscurity in the last twenty years to become top of the pops, and to extol their virtues would be preaching to the converted. True, there are still many trim gardens where neat, straight edges to the flower-beds are the ideal and where the soil between roses, herbaceous plants or shrubs is religiously weeded or hoed. But more and more gardeners are filling these spaces with foliage plants and ground cover, and most nurseries and garden centres now offer a good run-of-the-mill selection of hostas, heathers, periwinkles, bergenias, and lamiums. Some of these are so mass-produced that they have become banal, and for more distinguished plants, one must wander round some of England's imaginative gardens with a notebook and a beady eye, and then rake the lists of discriminating nurseries looking for stock. Sunningdale Nurseries, The Margery Fish Nursery and Will Ingwersen's Nurseries usually turn up with something special.

Some ground-cover plants fill space by forming clumps and others by sending out overground runners or underground shoots. Some have attractive flowers as well as leaves, but many are first and foremost foliage plants. There is a third category of shrubby plants, like heather, thyme, potentilla and *Iberis sempervirens*, which don't fill the ground, but cover it like a crinoline, but I have included some of these with my cushion plants and don't want to be repetitive – many of these categories overlap.

Of the clumpers, many of my favourites are shade-lovers, like the epimediums and pulmonarias. The epimediums have frail-looking, rose-tinted leaves which tremble in summer and rustle in winter, when they turn brown and papery, but remain on the plant. The tiny flowers are usually yellow, but there is a red variety, *E. rubrum*. The clumps are not only extraordinarily graceful but completely weed-proof. Another of the loveliest foliage plants, *Pulmonaria saccharata*, also prefers moisture or semi-shade, though it is not too fussy about it. After the pink-and-blue flowers die, in spring, the spotted leaves grow larger and larger until the small white spots become great white splashes; the leaves are almost evergreen, not dying off until after Christmas. Pulmonaria is no longer a common wild plant in Britain, but the verges of half the roads in France are thick with it at Easter time, and my stock has been built up from a few French plants brought home in a plastic bag. Other good clump-formers, now grown in nearly every garden where ground cover is used, are bergenias and hostas – the spectacular display of hostas put on by the R.H.S. at Chelsea in 1968 won many converts. Ferns are also satisfactory clumpers in the right garden, their modest greenery being much in the modern mood, but, though I have been careful to plant varieties recommended for a dry soil, they do not prosper with me.

Of the 'running' plants, I would not be without lily-of-the-valley, of which I have an inland sea under a tall weeping cotoneaster. I tried for several years to get them going without success, and then tried, for my final throw, planting them in a thick mulch of leaf-mould. They are now so rampageous that I have to cut them ruthlessly back, or they would take over the garden. As soon as the young purplish-brown shoots push through in spring, I feel my garden has its share of profusion.

Another favourite of mine, which grows in our local woods, is the common woodruff, *Asperula odorata*, a shallow-rooting bedstraw which will spread quickly in the poorest soil. If you are unlucky enough to have a lot of builder's rubble buried in your garden, as I have, and can manage to cover it with a thin layer of soil, woodruff will soon carpet it with whorls of fresh green leaves and starry white flowers in spring.

Other good running plants are the periwinkles, which spread by layering, of which I like *Vinca minor* 'Variegata' best – the larger periwinkles are too coarse. *Lamium galeobdolon*, or archangel, is another layering plant with very good foliage, a dead nettle with yellow flowers and serrated leaves striped with silver. It is a quick carpeter but insists on shade, the leaves losing their colour in the sun. A dead nettle which will stand more sun is *Lamium maculatum*, but it becomes very rampant and is not easy to control. The white-flowered variety is prettier and more manageable than the common pink-flowered form, but few catalogues include it. It's a question of getting a root from a foliage-minded friend.

For full sun, the dwarf alchemilla, *A. alpina*, is as satisfactory in its way as the large, cushiony *A. mollis*; it has tiny, silvery palmate leaves, which, like the leaves of *A. mollis*, hold glistening drops of water after rain.

For an instant carpet or edging in a sunny place, the quickest grower of them all is *Stachys lanata*, or Lamb's Ear, its shoots rooting almost while you watch, and so easily propagated that a single clump can be divided into twenty plants or more. It is an ideal plant for filling newly cleared ground, as it is easily pulled up when you are tired of it and are ready for something choicer. If you don't want the tall flower spikes, choose the non-flowering variety called 'Silver Carpet'.

The gardens of which the profusion and richness stay in my memory are always those with plenty of underplanting, edging and ground cover. Some of the best underplanting I have seen is in the garden of Cranborne Manor. Though there have been many changes over the centuries since John Tradescant worked here, the garden is still traditional, settled and mature, full of old-fashioned and aromatic plants which send up a sigh of fragrance on a summer's day. I can think of no other garden where you feel so strongly 'This is England'. Wherever there are beds, there is underplanting, so that, although the garden is on a thin chalk soil, there is the profusion of Paradise.

Roses and tall herbaceous plants are filled in with clumps of lavender, pansies, sweet geraniums and a wide variety of cottage pinks. The North Court, which is planted entirely with white flowers – there are even more varieties, I think, than in the White and Grey Garden at Sissinghurst – has ground cover of white *Lamium maculatum* and white pansies. And the herb garden, the kitchen garden and many of the rosebeds are thickly edged with clipped herbs, dwarf lavender, clipped rue and *Santolina chamaecyparissus*, or Lavender Cotton.

Another garden where the foliage plants are very beguiling is The Old Rectory, Sulhamstead, a garden which I make no apology for mentioning often because I think it is one of the prettiest in all England. This is a low-lying garden which is kind to violets, and many are grown as ground cover, of which the purple-leaved *Viola labradorica* is the most delectable. There are also many prunellas and bugles, and one steep bank leading down to a marshy dell is smothered so thickly with *Lamium galeobdolon* that no weed can find a foothold. To find any bare soil at Sulhamstead Rectory, you would have to go to the vegetable garden.

Creeping and Trailing Plants

Lastly, the gardener who seeks luxuriance will grow creeping and trailing plants, both of which look their best against a background of brick or stone. I wish I could get more paving into my own garden, for I long to emulate the long double herbaceous border at Sulhamstead Rectory. Here, the borders run either side of a flagged path, and many creeping plants are encouraged to spread from the borders over the flagstones, forming dusky shadows. *Ajuga reptans* 'Variegata', with variegated leaves and piercing blue flowers in spring, creeps out to form one pool of foliage on the path; *Polygonum affine*, with pink spikes of flower in summer and leaves which go scarlet in early autumn, forms another pool; and there is a pool of purple-leaved clover, a pool of violets, and many pools of creeping thyme.

When looking for creeping things, one should study the alpine catalogues, like that of Will Ingwersen's Nurseries, for this is where the smaller creepers will be found. Here are the rock campanulas, like *C. portenschlagiana* and *C. poscharskyana*, and a bewildering choice of saxifrages, and the prostrate potentillas and the creeping bugles and clovers and thymes.

Trailing plants, like creepers, look their best against something solid, like a terrace or dry wall, and many plants which are usually grown as climbers are happy to trail. Common nasturtiums trailing over a paved garden, rambler roses, jasmine or honeysuckle planted in a bed *on top* of a wall to tumble over it, or little trailing alpines in a sink, all have an effete, lazy charm, as though the plants were too spoiled and too beautiful to bother to climb.

Trimming and Feeding

When you have planted a big population of plants, of course you've got to support them. Weeding is much reduced in a crowded garden, but trimming and feeding are very important.

If you don't trim, your paradise becomes a jungle. All shrubs must be pruned as necessary and climbers must be trimmed and trained. After inspection of climbers in hundreds of gardens, I've come to the conclusion that the neatest and least unsightly way of training strong climbers, like roses and vines, on a house or wall, is to hold them with horizontal wires tied into vine eyes. Lighter climbers, like clematis, passion flower or honeysuckle, can be held by wall nails or helped up a tree or arch with an occasional plastic tie or piece of string. The self-clingers with stem roots, like ivy or *Hydrangea petiolaris*, of course, do the job themselves.

Clippers must be used freely in the profuse garden, especially in spring, when lavender, rue, santolina and low shrubs like *Senecio laxifolius* need a sharp shearing – don't worry if they look a bit naked for two or three weeks. And when your herbaceous and cushion plants get too overwhelming, you must divide them, for permanent planting doesn't mean a planting so rigid that you never take up a single thing.

And the profuse garden must be well fed. In theory, the permanently planted garden mulches itself, as the wild woods mulch themselves in nature. In practice, the garden is often asked to produce *more* than nature would attempt, and good gardeners enrich the ground when they plant with manure, compost, leaf-mould or bonemeal, according to the plant's needs; mulch the garden at least once a year; and give extra feeds to special plants. I have gone more fully into feeding principles in the following chapter.

There is quite an interesting sex distinction in the choosing of fertilizers. I have found that chemical fertilizers are more popular with men than with women, who are great compost-makers, and find a maternal satisfaction in pushing a trowel-ful of compost into every space they can find, like a nannie pushing Farex into a baby.

Provided you feed well, there is no need to fear that thick planting is asking too much of a garden. I am impressed with that phrase 'they're happy in company'. Some of the loveliest gardens in England prove it's true.

CHAPTER V

A Child's Guide to Garden Feeding

Science is a department of life where I am such a blind wanderer that I accept without question any helping hand. When I'm ill, I do what the doctor tells me. When a lamp fuses, I send for the electrician. On the scientific side of gardening, too, I would like to be able to follow the experts.

This, regrettably, is quite impossible, for there are many experts and they don't always agree. For every man who tells you to pack in bulky humus, another will tell you to shake minerals out of a bag. Some experts tell you to poison your weeds and others to rotovate them. Some are worm fanatics and others put down worm-killer. Some are mulchers and others are double-digging manure men. One has, in the end, as with bringing up children, to discard both Spock and Truby King and decide for oneself. Although most of what I do in the garden is scientifically meaningless, when I look at my soil and see how it has improved over the years and how many light brown lumps have turned into good black crumble, I think one should not despise one's own instincts. After many consultations with soil and horticultural experts (I must give special thanks to Fisons for much help and infinite patience), I have leavened their valuable and much-valued advice with my own experience and with that of gardening friends, and worked out a simple feeding plan *for the busy gardener*. 'Busy' is the operative word. The part-time gardener can't always do the ideal thing. He has to fit in his gardening with his life.

Mulching to Improve the Soil

Nearly all good gardeners mulch the whole garden once a year with organic matter, probably farm manure, compost or leaf-mould. The subject of this book is the modern pleasure garden, which is largely permanently planted. In such a garden, whenever plants are put in, the ground should be well dug and richly fed with manure or compost at several levels. Some gardeners also work in bonemeal at this stage for the slow release of nitrogen, and work peat in among the plants' roots. (Peat is not a food, but it encourages root growth.) In after years, feeding will be by mulching and top-dressing at surface level.

But at what time of year are you going to give your general organic mulch? Already, we come to a division of opinion. Mr Sydney Searle, a weather expert and horticultural consultant whose own garden impresses me greatly, comes down entirely in favour of an autumn mulch. His case: nature puts down humus in autumn, with the fall of leaves; the soil is warm in autumn and the worms and soil bacteria break the humus down more quickly than when the soil is cold; the mulch will keep up the soil temperature; there is bound to be heavy rain in winter, so there is no danger of the mulch keeping the moisture out – a serious risk if soil is mulched in spring and dry weather follows. The weather pattern in England seems to be changing towards drier springs, and light showers falling on a thick mulch may never get through.

The many experts who advocate spring mulching put their case as follows: the heavy rains of winter will leach away the nutrients in the mulch; and a mulch is pointless when the plants are resting. They need the food when they start to grow.

We now come to a crucial point. What are organic manures for?

It seems to me that their primary use is not to feed the plants but to provide humus, improve the structure of the soil and increase its ability to retain moisture. Manures and composts may be nutritious, but their food value is uncertain and one never knows what's in them. Does the load from the farm consist of horse, cow or pig manure or a glorious mixture? Is the straw content high or low? Has the heap lost most of its nutrients, especially nitrogen, to the atmosphere while you waited for it to rot? What's in the compost heap? I wish I knew. If one accepts, as I do, that organic manures are not so much for feeding, as to improve the health and texture of the soil, there is a strong case for an autumn mulch, *because in the autumn one has spare time*. Professionals don't realize how much this means to the amateur.

In spring, working with very little help, I am always chasing my own tail. I never catch up with all the spring jobs, with the rose pruning, the spraying, the clipping, the weeding and the blasted grass. In the autumn, once the herbaceous plants are cut down, I am itching for work, and spreading manure and compost is just the thing to keep me happy. I put a thick mulch of organic stuff over everything in sight and by spring it has vanished. I have already said that the quality of my poor chalk soil has improved amazingly, and I'm sure that all the bulky manure which has gone on to it has done good work. Gardeners on clay are just as enthusiastic about bulky manures; they improve every soil, making light soils more water-retentive and heavy soils more workable.

Top-Dressing to Feed

Feeding, obviously, is most needed in the growing season, and the more heavily a plant bears, the more food it will require. Most gardeners would agree that it is sound practice to give all the beds and borders a spring top-dressing of some kind. A sensible choice is a general, organic-based quick-acting fertilizer – you must use exactly the amount they tell you on the bag or packet, and no more. The job must be done on a wet day, for plants take their food in solution, they can't eat dry powder. If it doesn't rain, you will have to water or hoe the fertilizer in. Gardeners who object to 'bag stuff' will top-dress with manure, compost, or other purely organic matter, and they are the backbone of the spring mulch school. Some prefer to scatter the beds with bonemeal, but this is expensive in a large garden.

In the case of deep-rooted plants, will the nutrients of a top-dressing get down far enough? Yes, they will, because the top 2 or 3 inches of soil are the important layer to feed. Most plants, even trees, tend to feed with their surface roots; the deep leader roots are for anchorage. For instance, the feeder roots of an apple-tree work in the top 6 inches. The food will always work its way down. If you try to work your fertilizers in deeply, you will probably damage established roots.

'Spring', you may say, is a loose term, and so it is. It may be ideal to apply your general fertilizer in late March, when, in theory, soil temperatures should begin to warm up, but if the earth is still icy cold, you may have to delay.

What about further feeds? The ideal is certainly to give a second top-dressing about June to perennial plants which bear heavily and to beds where the plants are being changed, and bedding plants put out, but busy gardeners usually confine themselves to extra feeds for roses only. Roses bear so much that they really do need three feeds a year, one at pruning time, and the other two at 6- to 8-week intervals. A proprietary rose food, high in potash, is the best thing to use.

I have suggested a general balanced fertilizer for most plants because I am dead against the indiscriminate scattering of chemicals by amateurs. Few amateurs have the knowledge to diagnose and prescribe for particular deficiencies and needs – I certainly haven't. However, a gardener who is something of a chemist may prefer to select special minerals for special needs – the three most important elements that plants need for growth being nitrogen, phosphates and potassium.

What about autumn feeding? A relatively new, and, I believe, highly respected practice is to supplement the main spring and summer feeds with slow-acting autumn feeds. It is a traditional practice to plant in autumn with bonemeal in gardens where phosphorus is needed. Many gardeners now give slow-acting autumn feeds to grass on the same principle. Hoof-and-horn is a slow nitrogen-releaser, for gardens where nitrogen is needed, and is strongly recommended by dianthus specialists for sprinkling under autumn-planted pinks. Hoof-and-horn is often better than bonemeal for general use in chalk soils, which tend to be short of nitrogen.

Foliar feeding is another interesting innovation, but I think only the chemists and professionals are competent to judge its value. Mr Roy Hay has had spectacular results from foliar feeding in dry summers, but, with my limited resources, I dread the thought of something else to spray.

Then there is the question of grass – my bugbear, for I have far too much of it and it is not of good quality.

Grass is extremely greedy of water and nutrients. If one followed the advice of the gardening Press conscientiously, hardly a week would pass when one was not treating the grass and one would have a lovely lawn, but totally neglected flowers. A simple minimum routine for those who refuse to be tyrannized by their grass would be one spring feed some time in April and one autumn feed in September or October; a rather fuller programme would be one spring feed followed at 6-weekly intervals by two summer feeds, and the one autumn feed as before. The spring and summer feeds would be with a plant food high in nitrogen to promote green growth, and this should not be applied later than middle August. The autumn feed would be with a product rich in phosphate and potash to promote root growth and general good health. The two-feed system should not prove too taxing even for those who are allergic to lawn work, like myself.

There is another quite opposite system which greatly attracts me, practised by Mr Sydney Searle, who cuts his grass to $1^3/16$ of an inch, no shorter, and leaves the clippings down for humus, the grass needing no other food. The result, on a chalky Sussex soil, is a lawn as green and velvety as that of an Oxford quad. The objection is that the clippings cling to people's shoes and may get tramped into the house, but for lawns away from the house, this sensible and labour-saving method is well worth a trial.

Mulching for Protection

There is a quite different sort of mulching from the autumn feed-and-humus mulch, and that is a blanket mulch to preserve moisture in the soil and to keep out weeds, and this is invariably put down in spring. It must be applied when the soil is wet and the mulch itself must be damp. This system can, however, kick back. The mulch will prevent evaporation of moisture from the soil, but it will also prevent sunshine and light showers from getting into the soil, and every gardener must decide for himself on the weather risks – it can be maddening if, in a nasty spell of drought, there is a light shower which never penetrates. As a weed-suppressor, such a mulch is invaluable, and possible materials are manure, compost, lawn clippings and peat. Peat is impenetrable and sterile – weeds simply don't hook on to it – and is probably the best of all, making a particularly tidy coverlet for rose-beds.

To sum up: deep manuring when planting, an autumn mulch, a top-dressing of fertilizer in spring, *or* a spring mulch instead of the autumn mulch and spring top-dressing, extra feeds for roses, and as much grass feeding as you can manage, seem to me to compose a good straightforward routine for the gardener who has only one pair of hands.

CHAPTER VI

The Wild Garden

A wild garden should not be attempted by anyone with a neurotically tidy mind. It is essentially a romantic sort of garden, and the wild gardener must readily come to terms with nature, and not itch to trim every deadhead and train every tendril. The French, with their formal manners and logical minds, do not understand it at all, but the romantic English, and still more, the Irish, are masters at it. All over Britain and Ireland there are beautiful wild gardens with plants growing naturally (well, nearly naturally) in woodland, in pasture or by water.

One of the most perfect I have seen is at Haseley Court, Oxfordshire, a woodland garden planted like a Botticelli, with hyacinths, scillas, tulips, anemones, violets and all the bulbs and flowers of spring, to be followed in summer by sheets of martagon lilies. Another masterpiece of wild gardening is the dell garden at Sulhamstead Rectory, a tapestry of marsh plants in a hollow sheltered by steep, wooded banks thick with superb flowering shrubs, such as magnolias, pieris, azaleas and rhododendrons – I am sure that azaleas should always be planted in woodland; they are too exotic for the flower-bed. Another is the stream garden at The Old Rectory, Holt, in Norfolk, where a little brook winds between flowery borders of wild and garden plants democratically integrated, high-born hostas living next door to cuckoo flowers. These are three of the best wild gardens I know.

A wild garden does not have to be large, though a depth of prospect adds to the romance of it and a deep wood is more intriguing than a spinney. However, a small wild planting can be made of a stretch of rough grass full of chosen flowers left to increase and seed, and bulbs or informal flowers can be naturalized under a tree. Even if I had only a small town garden, I would want to find space for some wild corner or a flowery bank.

A wild garden is not a wilderness, as William Robinson, who virtually invented the wild garden a hundred years ago, said over and over again. It is a part of the garden where plants are naturalized and left to increase without disturbance. It is a difficult kind of garden to plant and establish – much more difficult to create than a rose garden or a garden of lawns and bedding plants – but once it is going and filled with the plants you want, the upkeep is comparatively simple, and gets easier every year. As your plants and ground cover grow, the weeding becomes minimal. The wild garden mulches itself and should not require much extra feeding. And it is never untidy in the growing season, for fresh plants and grasses come along to hide the dying foliage. If, in late autumn and winter, you dislike the sight of withering plants and scattered leaves, you should not be wild gardening at all. The wild gardener must have a temperament which enjoys the sight of nature renewing itself.

I am going to draw, throughout this chapter, on the advice and experience of Lady Harrod (wife of the economist, Sir Roy Harrod), who created the present garden at Holt Rectory, for it is a triumph of wild gardening with the two essential qualities – it is romantic, yet well-kept. Lady Harrod, who is a genuine working gardener, not a mere snipper of deadheads, has told me in detail how she made and how she maintains the garden, discussing her mistakes as well as her successes. When I first saw the garden only five years after she began to plant, it already had that settled, I've-been-here-for-ever look which good gardeners seem able to achieve in much less than a decade. She inherited mature trees and great drifts of snowdrops in the wood, but all the rest she made, stripping turf and tearing out brambles and clearing the stream herself.

The shape of the garden is conditioned by the stream which runs through it. No question of straight paths or axes. It is everywhere curved. The house is an 18th-century former rectory of red brick with a honey-coloured stucco façade and an elegant Georgian porch, and the garden flows round it, with paths and beds and stretches of grass in swirling shapes. It is not all wild garden. There are lawns, a terrace, shrub and flower beds round the house, a pond with tame ducks, a croquet lawn, an arbour, and a walled kitchen garden kept up in the old-fashioned style with a full range of vegetables, a bed of sage to go with Norfolk duckling and six beds of Norfolk asparagus. But the glory of the garden is the wild garden, which is in full view from the house, for a wild garden is not something to tuck away out of sight. Ideally, the cultivated garden should merge into the wild garden, part of which should be visible from the house, but not all – Miss Jekyll's woodland paths could be seen from the windows, but they would wind away into mystery.

The wild garden at Holt is not one garden, but a series of gardens. The main lawn leads down to the stream garden, which is lightly planted on the side near the house with the marsh plants which are massed on the far side. Simple plank bridges (no Japanese nonsense) lead across to a meadow garden, which merges in turn into a woodland garden, which slopes steeply uphill. There are also many small wild plantings – groups of naturalized flowers in odd corners and a colony of bulbs or other plants under every tree.

There are three aspects of wild gardening which one must think about and understand – the making, the maintenance, and the choice of plants.

The Making

This is the hard part, for the preparation must be very thorough, or nature will take over. All scrub, coarse weeds and rank grass must be dug out or they will strangle your choicer plants. If the ground is in really shocking condition, you may have to poison the weeds and scrub and wait a year before planting, but it is better to hand-dig if you can, for strong weedkillers will kill attractive things like ivies, mosses, clovers and ferns. The clearing should be done as quickly as possible, and extra labour hired if necessary, for half-cleared ground will very soon fill up with weeds again and revert to barbarism, and your work will be wasted.

If you are going to plant a wood, a dry bank, or the verges of a pool or stream, you must make a total clearance of nettles, brambles, docks, ground elder and other noxious plants. If you want a planting round a tree, it is best to dig a proper bed and keep it forked over for a year or two after planting until the plants are established and able to take care of themselves, when occasional hand-weeding should be all that's necessary. Even if you are attempting the simplest form of naturalization, which is of bulbs in grass, the ground should be prepared before planting and the coarser grasses and weeds like creeping buttercup dug out, or they will smother the finer grasses and the bulbs.

Having prepared the ground quickly, you must plant it equally quickly. Some gardeners plant with quick filling plants to keep the weeds out and gradually build up the planting of their choice. The whole large dell garden at Sulhamstead Rectory was planted with quick fillers in one week, though now the planting is varied and subtle. Plants like astrantia, yellow loosestrife and alchemilla are good quick fillers, for they spread quickly and smother weeds, but lift out easily when the time comes.

For the first year, nature is always only too eager to take over again. Lady Harrod failed with one planting at Holt because she took her eye off it too soon. She planted a gully with primulas and hostas, went off on a trip abroad, and returned to find that creeping buttercup had taken over and strangled the lot. Speed and thoroughness in the preparatory stage are essential.

Planting must also be done as thoroughly as in a flower-bed – deep holes, compost or bonemeal, watering-in and the full routine. The same goes for bulbs. It's no good shoving a daffodil into a socket of hard turf. It needs a roomy hole and a pinch of bonemeal under the bulb.

The Maintenance

The maintenance consists of weeding, clearing and cutting. A woodland garden will always require some hand-weeding – the job gets lighter every year as the ground cover spreads, but nettles, brambles and elder must always be controlled – and an occasional raking and clearing and collecting of fallen branches.

The most important work in a pasture garden is regular cutting and the most necessary tool in the shed is a first-rate mechanical cutter. The critical question is how often to cut. There are various schools of thought on this, and you must make a key decision before you plant. At what season or seasons do you want your wild garden to reach its peak?

If you attempt a constant succession of flowers, you will either never be able to cut it or you will chop down some of your flowers before they have seeded. One well-tried and satisfactory system is to have an early spring display, with things like anemones, aconites, crocuses, snowdrops and early narcissus, to cut the grass in late June or early July, when the bulb foliage has withered, to cut again in August, and to have an autumn flowering of crocuses or colchicums. The final cutting is in November or December, making three cuttings in all. The cut grass, being too long to leave on the ground, is cleared for compost.

The system followed at Holt is rather different. Lady Harrod finds that three cuts a year is not enough and that with so little cutting, the grass gets coarse. She also feels that the theory that grass must be left uncut until every scrap of daffodil foliage has shrivelled is overdone. So the first cut takes place in late May or early June, or as soon as the cow parsley has flowered (this follows the spring bulbs and is a great feature of the pasture beyond the stream). After that, the grass is cut about every two weeks in summer, less frequently in autumn, and the final cut may be as late as Christmas. The grass is *not* picked up, but is left on the ground as a mulch, and the quality, for rough grass, is exceptionally good. After the spring flowers and the cow parsley, there are some summer flowers, but they are kept in island groups so that the cutter can be steered round them. There are columbines, monkshood, campanulas, and colchicums, both in the pasture and under the trees.

The stream garden requires rather more work than the wood or the pasture, for the weeding and trimming must be done by hand and the ground is always boggy. But the work is wonderfully rewarded. The stream is almost theatrically beautiful, the further bank so thickly planted with water plants, both exotic and homely, from giant gunnera to Ragged Robin, that it takes a pretty thick-skinned weed to crash the party.

The Choice of Plants

What plants do best in a wild garden? It's not so much a matter of what will *grow* well (almost anything will) as of what will *look* well in a wild setting. A hybrid tea rose would look quite incongruous in the bohemian company of speedwell and cuckoo flowers, nor do fat hybrid bulbs, like Dutch crocuses or Darwin tulips, look relaxed among ivies and periwinkles.

But there are hundreds of plants which naturalize perfectly. The small bulbs and corms and species bulbs are the easiest of all, not only the obvious ones like snowdrops, muscari, daffodils, aconites and bluebells, but also the smaller tulips, *Gladiolus byzantinus*, cyclamen, species crocuses, *Anemone blanda* and *A. appenina* and martagon lilies. When choosing daffodils for naturalizing, it is important that they should be neither too tall nor too short. The large ones look over-bred for wild conditions and the small ones get lost in the ground cover – I myself have only just learned, after burning my fingers many times, not to fall for the exquisite miniature daffodils at flower shows which are really for the rock garden. The Tenby daffodil, *Narcissus obvallaris*, is an ideal height, and so is my favourite cyclamineus daffodil, 'March Sunshine', and the Lent Lily, *Narcissus pseudonarcissus*, (ridiculous name) is probably the best of all. Lady Harrod used to plant daffodils in drifts of one variety, but later decided that this was rather affected and veered towards a general mixture. She sometimes plants tulips singly, a Rembrandt tulip shooting up surprisingly from a mass of ivy.

Many herbaceous plants naturalize easily. Anemones, including the tall Japanese ones, hellebores, euphorbias, campanulas, columbines, epimedium, yellow loosestrife, poppies, marguerites, acanthus and paeonies can safely be left to colonize.

Simple climbing plants, like honeysuckle and *Clematis montana*, should certainly be used in a woodland setting. Ferns are ideal where there is enough moisture. Some evergreens, like mahonias, hollies and daphnes, will do well under trees. They often do better there than deciduous shrubs, for evergreens work in winter, when the trees are leafless and the light and rain can get through. Even elms, which provide so thick a canopy in summer that the plants below are usually starved of water, can be successfully underplanted with daphnes or mahonias.

But the greatest of all plants for naturalizing is the rose. Hybrid teas and floribundas are, of course, much too stiff, but the shrub roses, especially the species roses and the old-fashioned Bourbons and centifolias, have the right, relaxed way of growing. There is hardly a place, in sun or semi-shade, where rose species like *Rosa rubrifolia* or the climber *Rosa filipes* would not look well.

The wild garden at Holt includes the following plants, as well as many small foliage plants and ground cover plants:

The stream garden is the chef d'oeuvre. The stream flows from a pond which is half hidden in a mist of *Rosa rubrifolia*. The far bank is thickly planted with herbaceous garden flowers, wild flowers and ferns. There are phlox, hostas, monarda, astrantia, Michaelmas daisies, sweet rocket, astilbes, many 'wet-bob' primulas, like *P. florindae*, *P. denticulata*, *P. pulverulenta* and *P. japonica*, *Iris sibirica* and *I. laevigata*, which grows right in the water. There are the sensational orange *Ligularia clivorum* 'Desdemona', giant gunnera, rodgersia, *Crambe cordifolia*, water avens, borage, huge clumps of royal fern and billowing alchemilla. Mingling with these are humbler plants like mimulus, kingcups, foxgloves, comfrey, various primroses (a favourite is 'Garryarde Guinevere', pale pink with purple foliage), forget-me-nots, fritillaries, cuckoo flowers and loosestrife.

The woodland garden is a steeply sloping copse of mixed trees, including the beeches, elms and sycamores which are notoriously difficult to underplant. But by cutting down a few trees and trimming others to let in light and rain, Lady Harrod has been able to grow a wide range of plants. Planting was always started at the top of the slope, as plants tend to colonize downhill.

The wood starts the year by laying out a total carpet of snow-drops, and follows with Solomon's Seal, narcissus, prim-roses, violets, alliums, honesty, bluebells, periwinkles, foxgloves, and many of the wild flowers of spring and summer. There are also a few groups of hydrangeas, rose species, *Daphne laureola* and summer herbaceous plants like monkshood, cranesbill and *Campanula latifolia*.

The prettiest of the smaller wild plantings is a graceful old larch-tree on the lawn underplanted with *Cyclamen neapolitanum*. The tall blue perennial poppy, *Meconopsis betonicifolia*, was tried first, but few plants succeed under conifers, and it had to be moved to the stream border. But cyclamen seem to thrive on pine needles, and a small group, planted 'in green' (that is, in full leaf, which is the best time) is spreading rapidly. This cyclamen seeds freely, but Lady Harrod presses some of the seeds lightly into the ground to make doubly sure, and collects others and sows them in pots.

Another good naturalized planting is under a yew-tree, where hellebores, lilies-of-the-valley, acanthus, honesty and the scented *Cyclamen europaeum* melt together in a sea of ground-covering periwinkles.

One great beech-tree is underplanted with winter heliotrope, *Petasites fragrans*, but this is very rampant and must be kept firmly to a wood, and never let into the garden, where it becomes an ungovernable weed. A group of Portugal laurels is underplanted with *Hydrangea villosa*, hellebores, pulmonarias and *Hepatica triloba*, with sweet woodruff for ground cover. A holly is underplanted with mixed daffodils. Most of these trees are stripped of their lower branches to let in light and air, a valuable idea which I have copied in my own garden, clearing the lower branches from my chestnut tree, to the benefit, I hope, of the plants beneath.

Not many gardeners have a woodland and still fewer have a stream, but wild gardening can be practised in quite small spaces if you have a taste for it. What is needed is not only skill but also an equable gardening temperament. If you are always nagging at the garden, trimming this and tidying that, you won't enjoy it.

CHAPTER VII

The Garden in Winter

Dilettante gardeners love the spring and summer, real gardeners also love the winter, and I've joined the club. For years, I put all my efforts into my spring garden, and my daffodils and wallflowers and lilacs burst into facile bloom in April and May, followed by the roses, followed by nothing. Any mug can have a show garden from April to the end of July.

Then I began to be aware of the autumn garden and planted viburnums and cotoneasters for their autumn leaves and berries, and though I can't yet claim that they make a blaze of autumn colour or remind me of New England in the fall, they are well-established and have made a declaration of intent.

Now, I've grown to love the garden in winter. I am not a jetset traveller who can fly off to the Caribbean in November or take a cruise every January. I am usually here in this sodden island right through the winter, which I calculate lasts in England for thirteen weeks, from mid-November to mid-February. During this period, I want to enjoy my garden, and as my knowledge of winter plants improves, I find I am doing so more and more. It is a rather private sort of pleasure, for I don't think a cottage garden can ever be showy in winter. (I have to admit that this is the season when the formal garden of stone terraces, spaced cypresses and clipped evergreens comes into its own.) To the visitor who comes to visit us in January there may seem to be 'nothing much out'. But in the owner's fond eyes, there is a hum of activity. There is always something to cut for the house, always some tree or shrub whose shape is delightful to contemplate (probably from the sheltered vantage point of the bathroom window), and usually, unless the snow lies thick, some small, early flower.

I believe there are six distinct kinds of beauty and interest to be sought in the winter garden. There are:

The shapes and textures of deciduous trees when bare.

The beauty of evergreen trees and shrubs.

The beauty of evergreen foliage plants.

The plants which always flower in winter.

The early spring bulbs and corms which flower in winter in a mild year.

The plants which give one hope.

Deciduous Trees

When choosing trees, one is apt to think of each tree in full leaf and forget about its structure and its winter shape; yet most deciduous trees are bare for a third of the year. The best way of sizing up the architectural merit of various trees without their leaves is to take a winter walk through Kew Gardens or one of the other botanic gardens, or round some good forest or park or arboretum. Don't stare fretfully *down at the earth* on your winter walk, hoping to find some reckless bulb pushing through, but stare *up at the branches* against the sky.

One January day, I visited the magnificent pleasure grounds of Westonbirt School in Gloucestershire, which were planted by a great arboriculturist, Robert Holford, a hundred years ago. (I must make it clear that I am talking of the school grounds, and not of the adjacent arboretum, administered by the Forestry Commission, which is less of a garden, more of a forest, but equally fine, with picture plantings of many diverse trees to give the private gardener ideas and pleasure.)

I was shown round by the head gardener, Mr Robert Gates, who had worked at Wisley, who helped me with the identification of the trees and shrubs and answered an artillery of questions about hardiness and culture. Although it was pouring with rain, and we must have looked absurd tramping round under open umbrellas, I enjoyed my tour and appreciated the trees as much as if I had gone on a midsummer's day.

The comforting thing about Westonbirt is that it is not one of those annoying semi-tropical gardens sheltered by the Gulf Stream and never touched by frost. It stands high on a ridge of the Cotswolds exposed to every westerly blast. It looks a natural paradise, yet its problems are my own.

I found that many trees look beautiful in winter through their very bareness. Some excel because of their fine structure while others have beauty of bark or twig. That prince of gardeners, Mr Bowles, took such pleasure in tree-bark that he used to stand on a chair and scrub the trunks of his yew trees with a kitchen scrubbing-brush until they glowed 'a rich, warm crimson, especially after rain'.

Of the architectural trees, English elms, wych elms, planes, limes, oaks, ashes, chestnuts, catalpas, and the North American *liriodendron*, or tulip-tree, are magnificent in winter, though too large for many gardeners to consider. Specimen oaks have to be planted at least sixty feet apart, which puts them out of court for the small garden. The slowness of growth of hardwood trees seems to me less of an objection, for most gardeners like to plant something for themselves and something for posterity, on the loose principle of a spoonful of tea per person and one for the pot.

Of the large trees, the common chestnut, *Aesculus hippocastanum*, is one of the fastest, and walnuts are not too sluggish. After the first two years, when nothing seems to happen, the growth of hardwood trees increases in geometrical progression and becomes a pleasure to watch. I have often admired the unselfishness of Capability Brown's 18th-century patrons in planting so much for the future, but I don't think their lives were a total self-abnegation.

But the good 'shape' trees are not all large. Many are small enough for a cottage or a town garden, and of these, the weeping trees are outstanding. There are some wonderful weepers to be seen at Westonbirt – weeping beech, birch, elm, holly, hemlock, ash, mulberry, and, of course, exquisite weeping willows. Mr Gates recommended Young's weeping birch, *Betulus pendula* 'Youngii', with mushroom silhouette and silver trunk, as the ideal tree for a small garden. Other possibilities are *Pyrus salicifolia* 'Pendula', the silver-leaved Willow Leaf Pear; *Fraxinus excelsior* 'Pendula', the weeping ash; or one of the umbrella-shaped Japanese maples which have brilliant autumn leaves.

The deciduous magnolias are also impressive when bare. Walking round Kew one Christmas, I saw a *Magnolia soulangeana* with strong bare branches already swelling with fat buds. And a charming oddity of a tree which I recommend to eccentrics is the Cork-screw Hazel, *Corylus avellana* 'Contorta', which looks, in winter, as though the bedsprings had jumped out of the bed. Mr Bowles had it in his 'lunatic asylum', the corner of his garden which he kept for demented plants.

For smallish gardens, there is also the whole world of fastigiate trees, many of which are well-shaped. Most trees have a fastigiate, or upright, form, even the oak, *Quercus robur* 'Fastigiata'. As oak roots travel deep, and find their food far down, they can be successfully underplanted. I remember from my childhood that it was always the oak woods which were thickest with primroses in spring.

Many deciduous trees have another quality which makes them interesting in winter, curiosity of bark. The Snake-Bark Maple, *Acer pennsylvanicum*, the striped maple, *Acer grosseri*, and the peeling Paper-Bark Maple, *Acer griseum*, have bark of extraordinary texture which shows best when the leaves are down. Trees with outstanding coloured bark are the Coral-Bark Maple, *Acer palmatum* 'Senkaki', which bears a soft bloom on its branches, *Cornus alba* 'Kesselringii', a dogwood with purple bark in winter, and many birches and willows – the young willow wood may be green, yellow, orange or purple according to variety (Hillier's catalogue will sort them out for you) and you cut them back annually to get plenty of young, tinted growth. There are also the Mahogany-Bark cherry, *Prunus serrula*, and the red-twigged dogwoods, of which *Cornus alba* 'Sibirica', the Westonbirt dogwood, is the most spectacular, making crimson thickets in winter if the bushes have been pruned hard in spring.

Evergreen Trees and Shrubs

Evergreens are plants which arouse strong human reactions, and their popularity has see-sawed with different generations of gardeners.

When the botanist-explorers of the late 18th and early 19th centuries brought back new evergreens from the corners of the earth, it became the height of fashion to grow them, and exotics like the Monkey-Puzzle (introduced in 1796) and the Wellingtonia (1853) were Victorian status symbols.

Then William Robinson, that bellicose gardener, led a reaction, and, though he approved our native evergreens, yew, holly and the Scots pine, and admitted the claims of certain choice foreigners, he slammed many fashionable evergreens in harsh language, and there was a strong anti-evergreen camp lasting from Robinson's time until after the last war. Evelyn Waugh, searching for an expression of disgust to describe Hitler, called him 'a creature of the conifers'. And in sophisticated circles laurels were an object of derision.

Then the pendulum swung again, and evergreens became part of the great post-war shrub revival, so that now there is scarcely a garden without a planting of evergreen trees or shrubs.

It would be tedious if I attempted to list the many hardy evergreens which are readily available to the gardener, for they can be found in any good catalogue and, anyway, the task would keep seven botanists with seven mops sweeping for half a year. I will confine myself to a few personal comments based on observation of many gardens where evergreens have given me pleasure.

Of the broad-leaved evergreens, the Holm Oak, *Quercus ilex*, is the grandest, but is not widely grown in England except in municipal cemeteries and by the sea. I had never thought of planting one myself until I saw the majestic ilexes at Westonbirt, and then I toyed with the idea, but I am still only toying. It is a sombre tree.

Perhaps the broad-leaved evergreens are best when variegated, for the shading of colour takes away the heaviness. Variegated hollies make particularly brilliant shafts of light on a winter day. *Ilex aquifolium* 'Golden Milkmaid' is a striking variety with bright gold leaves margined with green, and *I.a.* 'Golden King' is patterned the other way round, with broad green leaves outlined in gold. *I.a.* 'Ferox Argentea' is a fine silvery holly to grow as a specimen, though too spiny for hedges – clearing up the clippings is too painful.

Another variegated shrub which illumines the garden when

the deciduous trees have shed their leaves is *Elaeagnus pungens* 'Maculata', with bright green leaves splashed with gold. As with other variegated plants, if a branch fails to variegate, you should cut it out, but not too soon, for sometimes a branch makes up its mind to toe the line when you have quite given up hope. This elaeagnus makes a pool of sunshine on a dark day. Another graceful elaeagnus is *E. ebbingei*, with dark, glossy, silver-frosted leaves with pale silver linings which shimmer when the wind blows. This is a tough and fast-growing shrub, a perfect screen or shelter plant, with the virtues of the common laurel but far more distinction, and with the bonus of tiny scented bells of flowers in the autumn.

Of the smaller variegated shrubs, *Euonymus fortunei* 'Silver Queen' is as pretty as any, with a pink tinge in the leaves in winter. It turns up at all the flower shows and is sold at most garden centres, but, for all that, it never seems stale or overdone.

The one evergreen which does not need the light touch of variegation is box. This perfect plant, tough but responding happily to the clippers, evergreen but springlike with its fresh new shoots, impressive as a tree but neat as a dwarf edging, could furnish the garden in winter single-handed.

To see box at its finest, I urge the reader to make a visit to Hidcote. The famous hedged gardens at Hidcote are usually enclosed by four hedges which are dissimilar, reminding one that irregularity is an element of great design. One garden is enclosed by three hedges of yew and one of box, the two greens enhancing each other. Another garden has one hedge of box, one of holly, and one of beech, while the fourth side is a stone wall. Box is also used in the famous 'tapestry', or mixed hedges, one of which is planted with no less than five subjects, box, yew, holly, hornbeam and beech. Topiary of box and yew is another feature of Hidcote; and makes me long to grow a topiary peacock or pyramid, or even a simple dome, before I die. The Hidcote topiary is not extravagantly artificial in the manner of 17th century topiary, but has a cottage charm. Miss Sackville-West described it as 'in the country tradition of smug, broody hens, bumpy doves, and coy peacocks twisting a fat neck towards a fatter tail'. How gratifying to have grown a smug hen or a bumpy dove!

In these suggestions for evergreen shrubs, I am afraid there is a great lacuna. I have had to leave out the lime-haters – the rhododendrons, azaleas, camellias and pieris – which I can't grow but which enthusiasts will say are the finest shrubs of all. It's better for me to pass them by than discuss them ignorantly, and to go on to the conifers.

Conifers, like broad-leaved evergreens, can brood heavily on the garden unless they are well chosen and well placed, and as you will probably be planting them for life, it is worth giving prolonged thought to your choice, thinking about the setting as well as the varieties. A plant which will look cheerful against mellow brick may look melancholy against West Country stone, and a group which will be feathery against open sky may be too solid with a city background. If you can get to an arboretum, like Westonbirt, or to a pinetum, like Bedgebury Pinetum, in Kent, it will help to clarify your thoughts. Bedgebury is an offshoot of Kew Gardens with magnificent mature plantings of an enormous range of conifers on a fine, contoured site; all the trees are well-labelled, so that it is worth taking a notebook and recording names.

This collection is rich in blue conifers, from the grey, smoky blues to the almost turquoise green-blues. There are majestic blue cedars and the pinnacles of many blue cypresses. Thinking in garden terms, I fancy that the larger blue conifers would need to be in a very grand, formal garden, for the tall blue columns and spires have a cathedral quality which might overwhelm a cottage-style garden. But small blue conifers, like *Chamaecyparis lawsoniana* 'Fletcheri' or *Juniperus squamata* 'Meyeri', are useful anywhere.

I myself, having been converted to conifers pretty late in life, and being still only half-hearted, have a fancy for variegated and golden varieties, but many gardeners consider them a vulgarity – crusty old Robinson called them 'monstrosities'.

I wouldn't want a whole copse of golden conifers, but a few of them sprinkled among groups of dark conifers do lighten the gloom. Many of the best cypresses and false cypresses and junipers have a golden or silvery or creamy-mottled form, or have young shoots which are gold in spring or summer, and some of the thujas have golden lights. I have a vigorous specimen of one of the golden prostrate junipers in my own garden, *Juniperus pfitzeriana aurea*, but unfortunately I made a dreadful boob in placing it, and it is growing so large that sooner or later it will have to come out. It is in a narrow bed with various low shrubs which it is threatening to smother, while one waving arm is trying to cross a grass path and invade a rosebed – a cautionary tale about the dangers of putting in a large plant without studying its habits first.

The one conifer about which I have no reservations at all is yew, which, perhaps because it is a native plant, enhances every English garden where it grows.

On the chalk downs where I live, yew is a common wild plant, and every cottage has its yew hedge and every churchyard its ancient tree. Yew is neither difficult nor slow to grow, and if you put in two-and-a-half foot plants in well-dug holes with some rotted manure, you ought to be the owner of a noble hedge within eight or nine years. I myself had forty yews planted in 1968 on an unpromising bank of solid chalk, and already there is a hedge of respectable size, which called, I decided one day, for a pair of couchant lions, or some other heraldic beasts, to finish it off in style. However, my dreams of grandeur evaporated when I started to look for them, for the cheapest pair I could find which I considered worthy of the hedge cost £400, so I shall probably end up with a pair of pseudo-stone pineapples.

Both English yew and Irish yew are very widely used in our district in ways both traditional and unorthodox, and I have deferred a fuller description of some of the best planting ideas to Chapter XII, 'Eye Witness'.

The other conifer of aristocratic bearing is also a British native, *Pinus sylvestris*, the Scots pine. There are not many in our district, but we are lucky enough to look out from the north windows of our cottage on to a fine, if windblown, Scots pine in the vicarage garden. Its tawny trunk, topped with a big flat cap of green needles, looks as warm in winter as a good fire.

Apart from conifers grown for decoration, the best of the utility conifers can give year-round pleasure. A thick hedge of clipped

Lawson cypress or *Thuja plicata*, or a group of Leyland cypresses grown as a screen, provide good winter furniture.

Evergreen Foliage Plants

It is easy to become a bore about foliage plants. They enter so many aspects of gardening that the same names are bound to recur. How do you smother weeds? With foliage plants. How to make rose-beds more interesting? With foliage plants. How to clothe the garden in winter? With foliage plants. One begins to think that foliage plants will do anything except light the bonfire and scare the sparrows.

I don't want to be a gramophone and I have referred to foliage plants under other headings, so I will confine myself here to a few skeleton notes on plants of small or medium size which stay green and above-ground through the winter. They include small shrubs, clumpy plants, creeping and climbing things.

Of the shrubby plants, my favourite is Jackman's blue rue, though a really bad winter may knock it back. *Senecio laxifolius* is my other love, wholly reliable and a great filler plant, making shrubby cushions on rough banks or in difficult corners, or flanking flights of steps. Its silver-grey leaves never seem to have an off-season. The Jerusalem sage, *Phlomis fruticosa*, fulfils the same sort of function, with woolly green leaves and handsome yellow whorls of labiate flowers in summer, but it is not quite so hardy. Helianthemums, which make low, shrubby clumps no more than a foot high, are totally hardy. I have never lost one, even in severe winters, and a plant which will survive in my cold garden will be hardy anywhere.

Many of the herby things are attractive in winter, and to me, the best is lemon-scented thyme, a long-lived plant which remains a glossy green all the year round. Common thyme, rosemary, lavender, sage and purple sage are also reasonably hardy, though I find it best to replace them every three or four years, as they get woody and straggly.

A more unusual evergreen plant which is a favourite of mine is *Chrysanthemum parthenium* 'Aureum', or Golden Feather, a cottage feverfew with lime green chrysanthemum leaves. It makes a pin-neat edging plant – the Victorians used it for floral clocks – but to keep the plant dwarf you must pinch out the flower-buds. If you don't, you get a crop of charming tiny white daisies on long stalks in late summer. It does not mix well with grey foliage plants, but needs a spot of its own.

The evergreen euphorbias are also fine for winter foliage, if you can provide them with a little shelter. *E. wulfenii* is the most handsome, but gets knocked by prolonged frosts. The native *E. amygdaloides* is hardier, a smaller plant, but 'showy' as the catalogues say, with red stems and red veins in the leaves. When handling any euphorbias, be careful of the milky juice, which is an irritant in a scratch or cut.

Of the more strictly foliage plants, *Stachys lanata*, the periwinkles, bergenias and lamiums are all perfectly hardy. So are many of the rock plants – the saxifrages, creeping thymes, veronicas, campanulas and polygonums – which keep their leaves. (*Polygonum affine*, with leaves which turn from green to scarlet to brown, is one of the most attractive of all creeping plants.) I wish I could say that the 'silver' plants, like the helichrysums, are equally hardy, but many of them are too tender for any but the most sheltered garden. I love them and grow them, but expect to have to make replacements every spring. The hardiest of all silver-leaved plants, in my experience, are the pinks, which are thoroughly tough. If they have been well clipped in summer in time to form fresh shoots during the growing season, they are among the best plants in the winter garden, making rich clumps in the borders or spilling over flights of steps. Watch for slugs, which like to creep under the clumps and chew the foliage on wet nights.

Cyclamen neapolitanum, which is usually thought of for its light butterfly flowers in autumn, is another beautiful winter foliage plant. Grow it in a mass, and the leaves make sheets of marbled green – a speciality at Hidcote. The epimediums are also loyal in winter, with halberd-shaped leaves which turn a rich brown and last all winter through.

When thinking of foliage plants, one must not forget the evergreen climbers. All the ivies are hardy, and I cannot think of a more cheering sight on a dull day than a wall covered with *Hedera helix* 'Goldheart' or the larger-leaved *H. canariensis*, two variegated ivies which I describe more fully in Chapter X. There is also an evergreen, or near-evergreen, honeysuckle, *Lonicera* 'Halliana', which I have found reliable and vigorous, and there are several varieties of evergreen clematis, but I haven't yet found space to try them.

Winter-Flowering Plants

To many gardeners, this is the nub of the matter. It is one of the greatest pleasures of the year to stroll round the garden on any tolerable winter day and see flowers in bloom – *real* flowers, not flower substitutes, like berries or patterned leaves. When all's said and done, twigs and barks and leaves are all very well, but there's no substitute for a good old flower. It is also gratifying to have flowers to cut for the house in the most unlikely weather. In some ways, it is easier to have a succession in winter than in summer, for in winter, the unexpected rarely happens – winter flowers have armoured themselves against the worst that nature can do – whereas in summer there can always be a freak frost or drought or tempest.

One of the treats of the winter garden is that so many of the flowers are fragrant, some of them as highly scented as carnations or roses. I have been told that they have been given this quality to attract such few insects as are about in winter, but I don't know if it's true.

The mahonias, the daphnes and the witch hazels give out wonderful winter smells. *Mahonia japonica* has tassels of yellow flowers which smell like lilies-of-the-valley and are impervious to frost. This is a bushy shrub, with large, pinnate evergreen leaves. *Mahonia* 'Charity' has a more upright manner of growth; like *M. japonica* it produces scented sprays of flower and is totally hardy. It is a weird-looking plant which I find hugely attractive; it is not so commonly grown as *M. japonica* and it is not always easy to find stock.

The daphnes are a more tender race, and by no means all are suitable for the cold garden. *Daphne mezereum* is reasonably hardy, but I am not over-fond of it, for I think the magenta flowers are a brash colour. I far prefer the richly scented *D. odora* 'Aureo-marginata' with clusters of pale pink flowers, each cluster nestling in the centre of a whorl of evergreen foliage, like a bridesmaid's bouquet. This daphne is certainly not fully hardy, but must have a well-made tent of bracken to protect it from frost.

Of the witch hazels, I prefer the pale yellow *Hamamelis mollis* 'Pallida', with sweet-smelling spidery flowers, to the more common deeper yellow *H. mollis*. *Chimonanthus praecox*, or winter-sweet, is another lovely winter-flowering shrub, but it is notoriously slow-growing. My own plant is only three feet high three years after planting, but it looks healthy, and I hope to cut its flowers in two or three years' time. I have given it one of my few sheltered corners. Meanwhile, a neighbour gives me a large bunch every winter, and the flowers last in water for three or four weeks, scenting the house. *Prunus subhirtella* 'Autumnalis', which is a small tree rather than a shrub, also has a sweet though fainter scent. The double white flowers are of bridal purity, and I prefer it to the pink form.

The winter-flowering viburnums are also fragrant, *V. bodnantense* 'Dawn' being perhaps the best variety, with large, soft pink clusters of flowers which come out in what gardeners call 'open' weather. They stand up well to frost, less well to rain. The shrub itself is not particularly shapely, but when the flowers are over, the leaves come very early and give an illusion of spring.

Though I love these winter scents, my favourite winter shrub has no smell at all, but it is so faithful, hard-working and graceful that one cannot expect this gift as well. It is our old friend, *Jasminum nudiflorum*, which will grow in the worst soil and the worst aspect in the garden and like it. Every year, I start cutting sprays of yellow jasmine for the house in November; the buds are then tight-closed, but they open in a few days in a warm room, and I am still cutting jasmine from the same bush in March. The flowers, like six-pointed stars, are among the prettiest in the garden, and their pale yellow is perfect, making the deep yellow of forsythia look coarse beside it. Though forsythia can be forced equally well in the house, I consider it an inferior shrub in every way.

Two other shrubs which just creep into the winter-flowering category are *Cornus mas*, an elegant dogwood with tiny yellow-green flowers which will, with luck, be out in February, and the quick-growing evergreen, *Garrya elliptica*, which is draped in mid-winter with long strings of catkins.

Most of the early spring bulbs must come into the next section, for they are often delayed into March or even April, but there is a handful of genuine winter customers.

Prominent among these are the winter irises (rhizomatous or bulbous), of which the incomparable *I. stylosa* (*unguicularis*) will often flower from November to March. Mr Bowles chose it as one of the two flowers he could not possibly do without, the other being *Chimonanthus fragrans*. It needs a sunny, well-drained spot, and once established, each clump produces an amazing number of lavender blue flowers with feathery markings of purple, yellow and white on the ridges.

The dwarf irises, *I. histrio aintabensis*, *I. histrioides* 'Major' and *I. reticulata* can also be counted safely with the winter flowers. *I. reticulata* is quite strongly scented for so tiny a flower, and if you cut a tightly folded bud and bring it into the house it will pop open in half an hour. There are a number of varieties in different shades of blue and purple, usually with little orange blotches. It is ideal to choose them not from a catalogue, but at one of the R.H.S. early spring shows.

Many of the heathers flower in dead of winter. I am not a heather-lover myself, but am forced to admit that a bank of rich pink *Erica carnea* 'Winter Beauty' can look spectacular in January. *Lonicera fragrantissima* is a genuinely winter-flowering honeysuckle, the flowers small but sweet-smelling, and some of the hellebores can be counted on. *H. niger* is officially the Christmas rose, but I have never got it out myself before Easter, nor achieved good flowers even then. But *H. corsicus* has huge apple-green bells which are always in bud, and sometimes fully open, in January.

When it has finished flowering, which will be months later, one should commit an act of faith and cut the flowering stems to the ground – a worrying thing to do, but you will find new shoots already sprouting.

The First Bulbs and Corms

The flowering of the familiar and well-loved spring bulbs and corms, like snowdrops, crocuses, winter aconites, cyclamen, scillas, is a movable feast. I have seen the same group of snowdrops in flower as early as January and as late as April and it is only in an exceptionally mild year that snowdrops can be counted as winter flowers. They are essentially joys of spring.

To the run-of-the-mill gardener, a snowdrop is a snowdrop and a crocus is a crocus, but the specialist will grow dozens, even scores of varieties, a few of which will flower so early that they can be included in the winter circle.

Alas, I am not a good enough plantsman myself to write with authority about snowdrop varieties; I have a mass of mixed snowdrops in my garden, and I don't know what half of them are. I am trying, by making a few small plantings each year of named snowdrops, crocuses and cyclamen, to learn more about them, and also to stock my garden with more of the early varieties. At present, I'm too ignorant to offer first-hand information, and the following notes have been put together after consulting specialist growers and writers. (For gardeners who want more specialist information on winter bulbs and other winter-flowering plants, too, I highly recommend an expert but readable and attractive book called *The Winter Garden*, by M. J. Jefferson-Brown.)

The growers tell me that *Galanthus nivalis* var. *cilicicus* is the earliest winter snowdrop, usually in flower at Christmas, but it is not an easy snowdrop to establish; nor is the long-stemmed early snowdrop, *G. elwesii*. But *G. nivalis* 'Atkinsii' is easy to get going. In a mild year, *G. caucasicus* and *G. byzantinus* should flower in January in a sheltered spot, to be followed by *G. graecus*, which comes out with the winter aconites.

The crocuses are less difficult for the amateur to distinguish, and I have proved to my own satisfaction that some of the crocus species and varieties of *C. chrysanthus* flower much earlier than the fat Dutch hybrids. *C. ancyrensis*, a small orange-yellow crocus, is the earliest of the yellow varieties, and *C. imperati* is a very early lilac crocus with striped flowers. Then come the chrysanthus crocuses of which 'E. P. Bowles' is my own favourite, a lemon yellow crocus with feathery chocolate markings at the base of the petals. In 1970, I had a little group of them in full flower when we were visited by a heavy snowstorm, which did not affect them in the slightest. After the storm, the snow lay on the ground for a fortnight, and they flowered serenely through it. *C. tomasinianus*, in shades of blue and violet, is another charming early crocus, which spreads fast. (Of course *C. laevigatus* is earlier than any of these, but it is an autumn crocus and may be over before winter starts.)

All these early snowdrops and crocuses have the merit of dying down before you need to mow the grass. They are the tidiest of all bulbs, and I try to stuff in a few more dozen every year.

Cyclamen specialists will tell you that there need not be a week from October to May without a cyclamen in the garden. In my cold soil, I have not achieved this, but I know of milder gardens where pink, crimson and white varieties of *C. coum* can be counted on for Christmas except in fiendish winters. I love cyclamen. They are beautiful, tough and prolific, and they remind me of the golden happiness of holidays in Greece before the Colonels. A sheet of autumn cyclamen among the ruins of the little island of Samothrace is a vivid memory, though it is twenty years since I saw them. We landed at Samothrace from a small boat on a sunny October day, and a string of mules was waiting on the shore to take us up into the hills to see the ruins. The mules trampled the wild cyclamen as we rode, and at first I tried to steer clear of the flowers, but there were far too many to avoid, and, anyway, I had no control over my mule.

Some chroniclers of winter flowers include *Anemone blanda* in the winter calendar but I think this is cheating. I would be glad of any reasonable excuse to write about this lovely flower, but it is a spring flower, and must stay in its proper place.

Plants Which Give Hope

There are a few plants which give one a purely psychological boost in winter because they shoot so early, while the old year is still dying, and I like to have a few in the garden to raise my morale when the days get shorter. *Sedum spectabile* is a classic example, shooting strongly in November, while the old chocolate-brown flowerheads are still clinging to their stalks. The hardy geraniums are also optimistic plants, putting out a mass of new leaves in early autumn when most of the border plants are in a state of collapse. The alchemillas do the same, but I know I am an alchemilla bore. Of the smaller trees, my favourite whitebeam, *Sorbus aria* 'Lutescens', makes strong shoots in autumn as a promise that the silvery leaves will be back before long. The rugosa roses shoot early, and an apple tree in November is always covered with cheerful buds.

CHAPTER VIII

Ruth Draper Time

The garden was a picture last week and there's going to be a blaze of colour next week, but nothing is actually out at the moment. Ruth Draper's famous act as a hostess showing her guests round the garden is established mythology, and even gardeners who are far too young to have seen it talk of 'doing a Ruth Draper'. Like Harry Tate's motoring act – 'one goodbye is quite enough' – it has given a phrase to the language.

I find there are two seasons in the year when it's difficult not to be caught with one's petals down, apologizing for the lack of flowers. There's a late-May gap and an early-August gap, when the garden seems to sulk after exceptional bursts of blooming.

The spring gap – tulips over, roses yet to come – afflicts most gardens for perhaps a week in a normal year, but it can go on much longer in a bitter spring, as in 1969, when the lilacs faded and the herbaceous plants refused to budge. There was precious little for cutting and even the professional growers were pushed to fill the stands at Chelsea.

The August gap comes when the first border flowers are over and the explosion of roses is spent, and one has been improvident about plants to follow. The garden looks dusty

and exhausted, there is not much in flower, and what there is
is yellow.

Yet there are some gardens so well-managed that even in a difficult
year, the two gaps are closed. For several years, I made a point of
visiting good gardens in late May and in early August, noting the
plants which were in their prime, and made a mini-catalogue of
trusty gap-fillers.

The Spring Gap

The most reliable plants to follow the April-May outburst of tulips,
wallflowers and rock plants are the May-flowering shrubs, for they
seem less liable to weather delays than the herbaceous plants. They
can keep to a time-table.

If you're on acid soil and have rhododendrons and azaleas, your
spring gap problem is already solved, but the rest of us must look
for shrubs outside this group.

Among the handsomest and most punctual of all May-flowering
shrubs is *Viburnum tomentosum*, either for growing in masses or
as specimens. I have described the ideal specimen viburnum, *V. t.*
'Mariesii', in Chapter IV. The very similar *V. t.* 'Lanarth' is equally
prolific of flowers in May, but is of looser shape and better for
massing. It will put up with very poor soil and mine are thriving
in a scruffy bank which consists largely of lumps of chalk and flint
and sub-soil. I would not have dared myself to plant anything
so handsome in such bad conditions, but Mr James Russell, the
landscape designer, suggested it and the idea was inspired. He
came to lunch one wet winter day and galloped round the garden
in the rain in elegant tweeds, disdaining my offer of boots and a
mackintosh, and scribbled down a few suggestions which looked
far too ambitious to me. As he was formerly landscape designer to
Sunningdale Nurseries, and now operates from a Vanbrugh house
in the park of Castle Howard, I feared he had been spoiled by years
of acid soil and skilled labour, but such is the eye of experience
that he saw possibilities I had not dreamed of. I planted a clump
of viburnums in the dreadful spot he marked, and they flourished

and I'm extremely grateful. Gardeners of the picture school who visit me in May have been heard to say 'Thank God you've got a group of something'.

Another ravishingly pretty May-flowering shrub is deutzia, which is surprisingly little grown, for it is a very neat shrub which is smothered every year without fail in small, starry flowers. I like all the varieties I have seen, but the best is *D. rosea* 'Carminea', which is no more than four feet high with arching sprays of rose-pink flowers which turn to mauve as the flower fades. Even in the dread spring of 1969, the deutzias in my garden were punctual, unaffected by eight months of icy rain.

The Canadian lilacs are worth considering, listed as *Syringa prestoniae*, for they bloom a fortnight later than most lilacs and are staunch gap-fillers. The bushes are a better shape than the familiar lilacs, but the flowers are smaller and haven't much scent, so I don't recommend them passionately unless you have a large garden with plenty of shrub space.

On the other hand, I find the earliest shrub roses indispensable. They come just when fresh blood is needed. The first to flower in my garden is always the Canary Bird, which makes a splash of butter-yellow flowers in May, the blossoms crowding on graceful stems feathered with ferny leaves. A Canary Bird rose in full bloom is one of the prettiest sights in the garden. They usually flower in their first season after planting, for Canary Bird can't wait to show off. *R. hugonis*, with paler yellow single flowers, is equally early, and another rose species, *R. rubrifolia*, is also at its peak in May. True, the tiny, insignificant flowers come later, but the haze of blue and red foliage which is the beauty of this rose is at its softest when the leaves are young. Of the modern shrub roses, the glorious spinosissima hybrid, Frühlingsgold, can be counted on for the same period.

Most of the tree paeonies, too, flower in May, and one should do nothing but stand with hands folded like a Chinese mandarin and contemplate their perfection for the few days of their blooming. In my garden I have four yellow-flowered tree paeonies of enormous size, *P. lutea ludlowii*, but as far as I'm concerned, it's four too many, for their season is brief and their greed is great, while their appearance in autumn and winter is quite disgusting. But they are beloved by my husband, so there they stay, and anyway it would take a more ruthless hand than mine to uproot anything so majestic.

Certain climbing shrubs are great gap-fillers, notably clematis, of which there's a variety for nearly every month of the year. *Clematis montana* falls neatly between the April-flowering *C. macropetala* and the large-flowered June hybrids. *C. m.* 'Rubens' and *C. m.* 'Elizabeth' are particularly exuberant, with rosy flowers which will climb to the top of a castle turret or smother an ugly town wall, curl over a rustic porch or hide the coal-bin. The two varieties are very similar, but *C.m. rubens* is a rosier pink, while 'Elizabeth' has slightly larger flowers. They are 'showy' without being coarse, and, grown on the front of a house will provide a spectacular opening number when visitors arrive for Sunday lunch.

A much more rarified climber which I long to try for its beauty in May is *Actinidia kolomikta*, the sort of plant which you see right across a large garden and cry out 'What on earth is that?', it is dressed so exotically. The foliage is variegated in bright pink, green and white, but not in an overall mottled pattern. Some leaves are all green, some all pink and others striped, as though some dotty artist had thrown a pot of rose-pink paint at the plant, with haphazard but exquisite results. I am not sure if I could grow it in my soil but would certainly try if I had the wall space. I see in Bean's Trees that it is a native of Manchuria and China, so probably it would take lime in its stride. On the other hand, there is no mention of it in F. C. Stern's *A Chalk Garden*.

But neither the shrubs nor the climbers are ideal for cutting (unless your *R. rubrifolia* can spare some branches) and for May bouquets for the house one must rely on early herbaceous plants and early irises.

A superb plant for cutting over several weeks is *Euphorbia epithymoides*, which clumps up so quickly that if you start with two or three plants now you will be supplying the whole neighbourhood three years later. Its large flat heads of sulphur-yellow flowers aren't everybody's meat but they are certainly mine, for I like flowers of sophisticated colour, especially in black vases. This euphorbia is a flower you don't have to 'arrange', it just falls into elegant attitudes.

Another cutting flower which comes at this time is the double red cottage paeony, *P. officinalis* 'Rubra Plena'. The fat flowers burst into flamboyant bloom just when the last tulips have blown over, at least a week before the Chinese paeonies; they look very good in the house with white sweet rocket. However, the cottage paeonies, like the tree paeonies, take up a lot of space, and I would suggest the dwarfer *P. o.* 'Anemoneflora' for a small garden. Its flowers are crimson and very satiny, with bright yellow stamens, and though this is an expensive plant and not widely listed or grown, it is worth the finding. When the flowers have blown, the plant is still attractive, the leaves smaller and bluer than the coarse leaves of the big red cottage paeony.

Another exciting perennial plant for this gap is *Dictamnus albus*, or Burning Bush, with ash-like leaves and spikes of white flowers. (There is also a purple variety.) It is usually listed as a June plant, but I know several gardens where it is always in bloom in May.

Irises are among the best of all gap-fillers if you choose the early ones and I strongly recommend the intermediate bearded irises from 10 to 28 inches high. These relatively new irises flower about a fortnight earlier than most of the tall bearded irises. They are very hardy, spread quickly, are less susceptible to rhizome-rot than tall irises and don't have to be divided more than once in five or six years, and as the colour range is literally iridescent, there is every reason for growing them. My favourite variety is called 'Green-spot', a 10-inch white iris with green spots on the falls. However, you can find tall irises for May flowering if you prefer them; choose from a catalogue, such as that of Wallace and Barr, where all the varieties are marked Early, Middle or Late.

Of the more fragile-looking flowers, the best gap-fillers I have seen are London Pride, Bleeding Heart and epimedium, all appropriate for the sort of flowers-in-a-wineglass arrangement one puts on a guest's bedside table with a trendy novel and a biscuit tin. London

Pride, *Saxifraga umbrosa*, is a fine plant dragged down by its name, for nothing could be prettier or more countrified than a thick planting on either side of a stone path under light trees with the sun filtering through. Bleeding Heart, *Dicentra spectabilis*, is the very archetype of a cottage flower, and the weeping stems of red heart-shaped flowers last surprisingly well in the house; while epimedium has found favour in my eyes since I discovered that there is a red form, *E. rubrum*, as well as the usual wan yellow.

One way of beating the gap, which I learnt in the Kent garden of novelist H. E. Bates, is not so much to hurry the summer flowers along as to prolong the season of the spring flowers by planting chosen varieties half in the sun and half in the shade. Mr Bates extends the season of hostas, polyanthus and auriculas by varying their diet of sun. Narcissus, too, can be stretched out until the end of May if some are planted in deep shade, and so can the spring hellebores and the fake forget-me-not, once called *Anchusa myosotidiflora*, now renamed *Brunnera macrophylla*. The new name turned up just when I had mastered every syllable of the old name, and was trotting it out like a botanist born.

The August Gap

The second gap presents no problems if you don't mind the garden being filled with yellow daisies. Some daisies are delectable, such as white marguerites, double cottage daisies and giant sunflowers with their kind, silly faces, but those lanky, hot-looking members of the order *Compositae* which take over from the delphiniums and lupins in most herbaceous beds in August fill me with languor. They are such blowsy flowers. Their whole air is *fin-de-saison*. Rudbeckia, solidago, heliopsis, helianthus, helenium, you can keep the lot.

Whether it's wet or dry, August is a debilitating time of year and I don't like flowers which make me feel worse. The most welcome plants in the garden are those which bring a fresh vitality – flowers in their first bloom, which is always fresher than a repeat bloom, and flowers fresh in colour. White flowers are particularly soothing on a sultry day, a cool hand on a fevered brow. I try to banish all yellow flowers in August to one part of the garden, to one of my dry shrubby banks, and to have as many blue, pink and white flowers as I can muster in the beds near the house. The only yellows I like at this time are the pale, lemon yellows, like that of *Verbascum* 'Gainsborough' and some of the achilleas.

There are quite a few herbaceous plants, other than yellow composites, which flower in early August. There are some shrubs of quality which are not yellow. This is the climax of the year for herby things. Sweet peas should be at their peak. And it is the big moment for bedding plants, which one must not dismiss too scornfully, but must look at with a dispassionate eye considering how to use them best.

The finest of all the August-flowering perennials is the Californian Tree Poppy, *Romneya coulteri*, which I have described in another chapter, but this beautiful giant is not an easy plant to grow and I haven't tried it myself. I have of course got some phlox, which have just the quality of freshness one wants in August – they could almost be spring flowers. I like the white phlox with a pink eye called 'Count Zeppelin', and the shell-pink 'Dresden China' and the ice-blue 'Snowstorm'. In a small garden there is not usually room for a mass of phlox, which are dull plants when not in flower, but quite a few clumps will provide flowers for the house all through August and will scent the evening air.

Two of the best blue perennials for August look rather like each other, though they belong to different families: *Echinops ritro*, the Steel Globe Thistle, and eryngium, or Sea Holly. Both have steely blue flowers which make an excellent foil for hotter colours, but I find the eryngiums, with their branching shape, the more decorative.

Another blue perennial which comes on just as the sweet williams make their exit is *Galega officinalis*, or Goat's Rue, a tall leguminous plant some four or five feet high with blue sweet-pea flowers and pinnate leaves often splashed with white. There are several varieties, but my own, with mauve-and-white flowers, is, I think, called 'Lady Wilson', and a surprisingly large number of people have wanted to know what it is and have asked for a root. It is excellent for cutting.

Monarda, or bergamot, is an equally reliable August border plant, a quick spreader and smotherer of weeds. I have the usual 'Cambridge Scarlet' and a pink variety called 'Croftway Pink', but the two have to be kept miles apart for the colours swear horribly. Either looks well near the sea holly. If you have space for much larger plants, there are two giants which flower at this time. *Acanthus spinosus* needs a bank or rough corner to itself, for, once planted, it is ineradicable. The very dark green deeply cut leaves were the model for the sculptured leaves of Corinthian capitals, and the huge prickly spikes of purple and white flowers make formidable sentinels. The other tall plant is more manageable, *Macleaya cordata*, or Plume Poppy, grown chiefly for the large glaucous leaves which grow all the way up the 8-foot stalks.

In a shady or dampish part of the garden, the astilbes should also be in flower, a plant beloved by every one of my friends, but for which I feel an irrational aversion. I have always seen it growing in pleasant natural places beside streams and pools, but somehow astilbes make me think of palm courts and tea-time music.

Searching for white flowers for the border, one must not forget the August lilies. July is the great month for lilies, but the lily gardener can still find varieties to fill the August gap. *L. regale* will probably be over, but *L. speciosum* is an August lily of great beauty. The type is white but there are varieties in a spectrum of exotic colours, and some have spots and others long stamens which tremble like antennae. *Galtonia candicans*, of the lily tribe though not a lily, will also flower for most of the month, like a tall white bluebell. It looks rich and rare, but is an easy bulb to grow, and should be planted in clumps in the border or among shrubs and left to increase.

The gap is a flourishing season for the labiate as well as the composite plants, and many herbs and scented things like lavender, nepeta and the decorative sages are at their best. I am mulish about lavender, being the only gardener in England who does not think that the dwarf 'Hidcote' variety, with deep purple flowers, is the choicest one to grow. Even if I plunge my nose into this lavender, risking scratches and bee stings, I can detect no smell at all, and I prefer the 'Folgate' variety, which is also dwarf, with traditional soft blue flowers and the true lavender smell. Nepeta is an under-rated plant, giving many weeks of neat foliage and lavender-blue flowers which are cool and serene in hot weather. And many of the aromatic sages, including the ordinary culinary sage, flower in August. The oriental sage, *Salvia virgata* 'Nemorosa', has blue-lipped flowers nestling in violet bracts and the scent of Greek islands in the sun. *S. turkestanica* is another pleasant August variety, with white flowers and pinkish bracts.

If you are well endowed with wall space, you can have climbers, too, refreshing the August scene. One of the best honeysuckles, the 'Late Dutch', *Lonicera periclymenum* 'Serotina', with cream and crimson flowers, begins to flower in August and there are any number of August-flowering clematis. There are also some climbing roses, like Mermaid and New Dawn, which start to bloom in late July or early August with a size and freshness of flower which repeat bloomings never muster. And to me, sweet peas count as climbers, as I still grow them up tall pea-sticks in the old-fashioned way. But most of the gardeners I know prefer the 'Knee-hi' sort grown as border plants, and I must be less stuffy and try them next year.

August shrubs, like August flowers, tend to be yellow. It's high noon for the potentillas, and *Hypericum patulum* 'Hidcote' is the undoubted lord of the August garden. This is, I admit, an indispensable shrub, so hardy is it and so prodigal of flowers, but I don't want a lot of it adding to the general plague of yellow fever. I much prefer a blue-flowered shrub, *Hebe* 'Midsummer Beauty', which has mauve-blue flowers in wavy spikes and thick, but not leathery, evergreen leaves. This hebe feels the cold, but though it may look pinched in a bad winter, it should revive safely in the spring. It is a shrub of most elegant shape, quite good enough for the mixed border. I can't say the same of the Tree Hollyhock, *Hibiscus syriacus*, but its trumpet flowers are a knock-out in August, white, blue, crimson or mauve, each with faint purple veins and a purple eye. At this season this normally dim shrub takes on a rich, prosperous air and should, one feels, be spending the dog days in some smart Mediterranean resort. Of course one must not be without a few buddleias, scented, reliable, *and not yellow*.

What about bedding plants? In August, if ever, they will come into their own, for they are born gap-fillers, designed to be reared out of sight and brought on as a ready-made show. Yet many of us plant them apologetically, so strongly have taste and fashion swung against formal gardening and the plants which carpeted Victorian flower-beds; and they are often so hideously used, flaming orange marigolds with fiery petunias making a fearful blaze.

I find that there is only one bedding plant which blends well with permanent planting, and that is the tobacco plant. I cannot have too many of these accommodating plants, which I usually buy as seedlings in boxes at market stalls. They scent the garden and the house all through August and September, and fill every gap in the flower-beds with their branching sprays. For all their apparent fragility, they don't need staking, but stand up to the roughest storms. And they look so natural that you can put them in the border, the shrubbery or the rose garden with perfect confidence that they will know how to behave.

The other bedding plants, even dahlias, are bad mixers. They must be grown on their own and can look very charming thickly massed on either side of a cottage garden path. But the more I see of bedding plants, the more I believe that in the modern garden their true place is in pots or tubs.

Pot and tub gardening is becoming increasingly popular not only with those who are limited to roof or balcony gardens, but also with gardeners who have plenty of space. The owner-gardener, always short of help, finds it convenient today to plant most of his garden permanently and to grow a few choice, tender, annual or biennial things where he can keep an eye on them – in pots near the house. It is hell to water a whole garden with a hose, but painless to water a few precious plants with a can. Impossible to bed out large areas, but simple enough to do a little potting on the terrace. And pots or tubs provide the neat, confined background which bedding plants require. Nothing looks more awful than a pelargonium placed to fill a space in the herbaceous border.

In August, if ever, one hopes to have a terrace life and to enjoy one's garden, not to be its victim. Cool drinks, well-loved friends, a show of flowers and a rest from heavy labour are what the soul requires at the end of summer. Pots and tubs of long-lasting petunias, begonias, pelargoniums, fuchsias, pansies, lobelias and other bedding plants, and perhaps also of lilies and hydrangeas, are then the perfect decoration. Ruth Draper's embarrassed hostess can't have known about pots and tubs.

PART III

Special Plants

CHAPTER IX

A Rose Catechism

Many millions of words have been written about roses. Poetic words about their beauty and their history and practical words about mulching and pruning and summer feeds. But there are still some questions which are not often publicly asked or answered though they nag at intervals at the back of the gardener's mind. For instance, my husband and I had a painful argument one summer as to whether or not to deadhead the rugosa roses. *He*, a man who is as much a menace with a pair of secateurs as a scissor-happy hair-dresser, said we would get no second flowering if we left the deadheads on, and *I* wanted the huge autumn hips. We had to wait for a solution until we next saw Mr Lanning Roper, who told us to leave the roses, like Frau Dagmar Hastrup, which have hips which are part of the fun, and the rose species, like *Rosa rubrifolia*, which have beautiful hips and won't flower twice, anyway; but to deadhead our hedge of Sarah van Fleet, which flowers far better with summer pruning.

As problems of this kind, which are not immediately solved by reference books, occur constantly to the rose gardener, I have written this chapter in question and answer form. The first nine of the questions below were answered for me by Mr Harold Hillier, of Hillier's of Winchester, who list more than six hundred roses in their catalogue. I spent a wonderful day in his company touring the celebrated nurseries, alternately asking questions and pausing to be dazzled by the roses and specimen shrubs. The remaining questions are answered from my own observation and experience, gained in my own garden and on my travels. Several concern the flowering season of roses, which concerns me very much, as few gardens can afford to give space to roses, however sumptuous, which flower for only three weeks. By the way, I have, throughout this book, omitted the inverted commas which should technically enclose the names of cultivar roses. Most of the names are so familiar that it would be an affectation for an amateur like myself to dress them up with punctuation. 'Caroline Testout' and 'Madame Butterfly' look like characters in a pre-war gossip column: Major 'Fruity' Metcalfe was present as was Mr 'Boofy' Gore.

Here are the questions I put to Mr Hillier.

More and more of us are growing shrub roses today, often as specimen shrubs in a lawn. How do you feed a rose planted in grass?

It's impossible to feed the roots properly *through* the grass. The rose takes its food in solution, and if you turf right up to the rose, the greedy grass will take all the food and most of the rain water and will prevent aeration of the soil. For the first two or three years after planting, it's essential to cultivate round the rose a clear circle of at least three or four feet in diameter, while a group of roses needs a larger circle. If you don't do this, the rose will be starved, and I have seen hundreds sicken for this reason. Later, the roots will find food and moisture more easily and you can underplant if you wish, but in the best gardens, you will usually find that enough soil is always left clear to allow feeding and watering.

At what age is a rose too old? Do you believe in changing one's plants fairly frequently?

Age is related to pruning and the nature of growth. Roses which are pruned often and drastically, like hybrid teas, usually have no more than from six to twelve years of good life. After that, it may be time to put them down.

Climbers and rose species can go on for thirty or forty years or more – I remember a Climbing Caroline Testout on my grandfather's house which was at least forty years old. If it had been pruned hard, like a hybrid tea, its life might have been shorter. It is also possible that very free-flowering roses work too hard and wear themselves out, and I have a theory that a rose grown on its own roots may last longer than a grafted rose. As a rule of thumb, if a rose looks as though it has had it, take it out.

How do you like to see roses trained and grouped?

One must remember that roses cannot claim much winter beauty, so I would like to see more roses grown as shrubs in association with other shrubs, especially evergreens. And I like rose species and hybrid musks, like the double white Prosperity, mixed in herbaceous borders.

I look all the time for roses with good winter foliage, particularly for hedges, so I like the hybrid musks, which are semi-evergreen, the foliage persisting until New Year. I also like roses in a mixed hedge, perhaps with thorn and maple, though I know it is difficult to get them established. I find climbers difficult to place, as I don't like artificial supports and one soon runs out of wall space and old trees. Unless you have a definite space earmarked for a climber, get a shrub rose instead.

In a garden where the soil is unsuitable for hybrid teas, which roses would you recommend for cutting?

Many of the floribundas cut well, especially Queen Elizabeth, the coral-coloured City of Leeds, Elizabeth of Glamis, Honeymoon, Rosemary Rose, John Church, Europeana and the peach-coloured Violet Carson. Some of the modern shrub roses can be cut, like the brilliant pink Elmshorn and the bright red Kassel. So can some of the rose species, because of the beauty of their foliage, like *R. rubrifolia* and *R. willmottiae*, which has fern-like scented leaves.

Which roses would you recommend for a cool, wet part of Britain?

Roses are strong plants and the following are a mere fraction of the many which will stand up to the worst of our climate. Of the hybrid teas, there are Fragrant Cloud, King's Ransom, Mischief, Super Star, Wendy Cussons, Madame Butterfly, Grandpa Dickson.

Of the floribundas, Iceberg, Evelyn Fison, Rosemary Rose, Queen Elizabeth and Orangeade. Of the shrub roses, the rugosas are good, like Blanc Double de Coubert, Roseraie de l'Hay and Sarah van Fleet, and so are the hybrid musks, Cornelia and Penelope. Most of these will have good foliage as well as good flowers even in a wet season. So will the climber, New Dawn, which has superbly polished leaves which never go musty.

Which white roses do you recommend? So many mildew easily or go brown in wet weather.

Frau Karl Druschki is one of the greatest of the classic white roses, and, of the newer roses, Iceberg is a strong rose which has come to stay. Seagull is a sturdy white rambler, Blanc Double de Coubert is a perfect shrub rose in every way. A very fine climber is 'Kiftsgate' form of the Chinese rose species, *Rosa filipes*, which climbs to a great height and flowers prodigiously even in the poorest soil.

What developments in rose breeding do you hope to see?

I would like a 10-year truce with *no* new roses while we take stock. There are far too many new roses every year of which only a few will still be grown six years later.

I cannot see that there is anything more to be done with colour, but I would like to see more work done on disease-resistance – a very important quality. I think we need more hybrids with strong species blood. Then there could be more work on dual-purpose roses like Frau Dagmar Hastrup, with attractive fruits as well as flowers. And more work on foliage colour, perhaps using rubrifolia parentage, particularly on improving the colour of the unfolding leaves. There could even be more work on thorns – there is a fine rose species, *R. omeienis pteracantha*, which has beautiful curved crimson thorns. I also think we should consider selling more roses on their own understocks to reduce suckering. All this would interest me more than yet another 'salmon rose deepening to flame'.

Are diseases, especially blackspot, getting more prevalent?

There is certainly a greater danger of blackspot with the reduction of air pollution, and perhaps some roses are becoming immune to sprays. Then, many gardeners spray once or twice at the beginning of the season and then give up, but I am afraid this is not enough

– spraying has to be kept up every three weeks all through the summer. That is why I am keen on research to get strong, resistant strains with species blood.

Which are the best climbers for growing up trees?

The most prolific is the *Rosa filipes* I have mentioned. And I like Mermaid, with its large, single primrose yellow flowers in late summer, and Wedding Day, which turns from cream to white to pink, and is probably the highest climbing variety of all.

The remaining questions are answered from my own experience and from that of rose-growing friends.

Many of the shrub roses, like Frühlingsgold, have one glorious flowering and nothing more, which is wasteful in a small garden. Which can be counted on for a continuous flowering or a second crop?

Most of the rugosa roses flower over a long period. The richly scented pink, semi-double Sarah van Fleet is almost continuous throughout the summer, and so are the picotee-flowered rugosas, F. J. Grootendorst and Pink Grootendorst, with clusters of small fringed flowers. After the first flush, Blanc Double de Coubert, the single pink Frau Dagmar Hastrup, dark red Mrs Anthony Waterer and the double purple Roseraie de l'Hay will flower intermittently through the summer. (All the rugosa roses are highly resistant to disease and are good for rose hedges, as they need little or no support.)

Many of the Bourbon roses are perpetual or recurrent, notably La Reine Victoria, a mauve-pink rose with a perfect cup-shaped double flower which goes on well into the autumn. Zéphirine Drouhin, with cerise flowers, which has now surprisingly entered the list of best-selling roses, is perpetual, and so is Souvenir du Docteur Jamain, the most velvety of the purple roses. The damask rose, Ispahan, with fold upon fold of pink petals, can be counted on for many weeks.

Of the modern shrub roses, Maigold, an apricot coloured rose with a cocoanutty scent, gives a massive first flowering and a repeat show in late August. Nevada will usually produce some huge creamy single flowers after the first June display. The single

Dortmund, with trusses of red flowers with a white eye, starts late but continues into autumn, a very strong rose, indifferent as to soil, but horribly thorny; even if you wear leather gloves when you handle it, the thorns will manage to penetrate the seams. And one should not forget that some roses, like the rose species, *Rosa xanthina* and *R. rubrifolia*, have such beautiful leaves that the short flowering period is relatively unimportant.

In very dry weather, it is important to try to water regularly roses from which you expect a second display. I found this with Maigold one dry summer, when the rose which I watered did far better than the rose which was just beyond the reach of the hose.

Which of the climbers and ramblers give value over a long period?

A stern decision must be taken by every gardener as to whether space can or cannot be found for roses which are perfection for three or four weeks only. I mean roses such as Paul's Lemon Pillar, which gives a profusion of large, superbly shaped white flowers for a short time and not even one stunted bud thereafter; and beautiful, rich-scented Albertine, which gives at best three or four weeks of bloom and no repeat performance. In a large garden, it would be unthinkable to sacrifice either, but in a small one, the perpetual climbers must surely be given preference. Of these, I would put New Dawn at the top, which has all the virtues of its ancestor, Dr van Fleet, but has glossier leaves and seems to flower for ever; next, Madame Alfred Carrière; the deep red Guinée; the very profuse, but scentless, Paul's Scarlet; creamy Albéric Barbier; and Wedding Day. Pink Perpetué, with clusters of carmine flowers, will bloom for months. Golden Showers is a long-flowering yellow rose. Climbing Caroline Testout will give an encore.

Talking of flowering performance, a rose expert, Mr Robert Lea, in Cambridgeshire, conducted a three-year experiment in 1966, 1967 and 1968, counting the numbers of blooms produced by a selection of well-known roses over the five months between June 1st and October 31st. Of the floribundas, Iceberg, Marlena, Sarabande, Hobby, Dorothy Wheatcroft and Lili Marlene came out highest in that order, and of the hybrid teas, Stella, Ballet, Buccaneer, Super

Star, Uncle Walter and Peace. Outside these categories, the hybrid musks Felicia and Penelope scored highly.

Are there any roses which are happy on a north wall?

Many roses will do well without sun so long as they are not exposed to the north wind. Madame Alfred Carrière will bear plenty of creamy noisette flowers on a north wall. New Dawn should do well and so should the great climbing rose, Mermaid. An arctic winter might cut back the latter, but it would recover. Gloire de Dijon is considered a good rose for any aspect, and so is Albertine, though some experts say that Albertine should be grown on a trellis, not on a wall. I have two on my cottage, grown directly on the wall, and both are vigorous, indeed, too much so – two Albertines on one small house are frankly a mistake.

Which of the floribunda roses grow like real roses, not in trusses of hectic, shapeless flowers?

Rosemary Rose is faultless, with double, quartered scented flowers, red foliage and all the charm of an old-fashioned rose, to my mind the best of all red floribundas. Iceberg is a *real* rose, and so are Ice White, yellow Honeymoon, creamy Gruss an Aachen, warm pink Plentiful, the double mauve Magenta, sometimes classed as a musk rose, and the tall Queen Elizabeth, with pink clusters of scented flowers of so pure a shape that the most romantic gardener could not criticize her. There is also a charming new shell-pink double rose called Anna Louisa which I saw when touring a rose nursery, but I have no experience of her in the garden.

Is the rose garden losing its smell?

No. If your roses don't smell, you are choosing the wrong roses. Go round any of the great gardens on a warm June day, and you will be knocked over by the scent of roses.

Of the old-fashioned roses, musk roses, Bourbons, damasks, centifolia roses and gallica roses are heavily fragrant. It is impossible to choose a few from so many, but I will just drop the names Madame Isaac Péreire, Ispahan, The Old Cabbage Rose, Madame Hardy, Souvenir de la Malmaison, *Rosa alba* Queen of Denmark.

Of the climbers – again, an arbitrary choice – Albertine, Mme. Grégoire Stachelin, Guinée, Souvenir de Claudius Denoyel.

Of the hybrid tea roses – Etoile de Hollande, Madame Butterfly, Lady Hillingdon, The Doctor.

Even modern post-war roses can be cleared of the charge of lacking scent, though some are crude in colour or insensitive in shape. Constance Spry, Iceberg, Queen Elizabeth and Dearest are among many which have charm of form and have inherited the old rose smell.

What are the advantages of rose species?

The wild roses, which come mostly from China and the Far East, have single flowers of a touching and innocent beauty which some gardeners think the richest hybrid cannot equal. It is the beauty of a young girl against that of a sophisticated married woman. Most of them flower brilliantly once in a season, but have arching stems and fern-like foliage which make them worth their place when the flowers are over. Some, like *R. moyesii*, have attractive hips in autumn. All of them are strong, most will settle in any soil, and they need little pruning.

Specialist catalogues list dozens of these primitive roses. Specially recommended: *R. moyesii*, with blood-red flowers, *R. willmottiae*, with lilac-mauve flowers, *R. rubrifolia*, with purple foliage and tiny pink flowers, the climbing white *R. filipes, R. farreri persetosa*, with the triple blessing of pink flowers, coral hips and purple autumn foliage, and the May-flowering bright yellow rose, *R. xanthina spontanea*.

How can one liven the fearful dullness of rose-beds when the roses are not in bloom?

You can, as Mr Hillier suggests, plant roses with other shrubs or in mixed borders. If you prefer them in rose-beds (and hybrid teas are best planted on their own), then give the beds a thick foliage edging. One of the prettiest edgings is *Berberis thunbergii* 'Atropurpurea Nana', a dwarf berberis with purple leaves, but it is expensive to buy in quantity. Clipped box, plain or variegated, is another charming edging, not cheap, but practically eternal. Much less expensive are silver plants, like *Stachys lanata* 'Silver Carpet', or clipped dwarf lavender or lavender cotton, all easily propagated from cuttings. 'Cuttings' is perhaps too grand a word for *Stachys lanata*, as you just pick a piece, stick it in the soil and it roots.

You can also partially underplant roses with clump plants like pinks, but it does make feeding and watering more difficult.

It also helps if you choose roses with good foliage, and mix roses which have different coloured leaves, like red-leaved Rosemary Rose with green-leaved Iceberg.

Which roses will grow well in chalk?

A great many do well, for they appreciate the drainage. The tag that 'roses like clay' has, I think, been misunderstood. They like best of all a rich, well-drained loam, or a clay which is not so heavy that it becomes waterlogged in winter, for they cannot bear wet feet. They do well enough in chalk, for they have no dislike of lime, but they want more food than a chalk soil naturally provides, so it must be heavily boosted with manure or compost. For varieties for chalk gardens, turn to Chapter XI, *Gardening on Chalk and Lime*.

What are the best ways to support climbers, ramblers and floppy shrub roses?

The best of all backgrounds for climbers and ramblers is a mellow brick or weathered stone wall, and the best means of holding them there is with horizontal strands of wire looped into vine eyes – this is neater than a peppering of wall nails. But only the lucky few have wall space, apart from the walls of the house, and after that, one must consider pergolas and arches. I can't say I like pergolas – they belong to a day-before-yesterday period of architecture for which it's hard to feel affection – but if you want your garden to drip with climbers and ramblers, no other prop gives so much perpendicular support. In a small garden, iron hoops or arches covered with ramblers can have a rustic charm.

Alternatively, climbers can be grown up trees or up a 'host' shrub. I like them up trees, when it is quite clear that the tree is a living support, but a rose interwoven with a shrub can look very unnatural. Does one really want a coniferous shrub to be, apparently, the parent of pink flowers?

Another sort of support for climbers is a tripod or obelisk of wire or metal, which is not obtrusive when the rose has got going; these are much used at Hidcote.

When starting a rose up a tree, or any perpendicular support, it is important to train it firmly for the first few feet. The best way is to tie your rose quite tightly to the trunk (or support) with parallel bands of string, as a butcher ties a rolled, boned joint of beef. The side shoots and upper branches can look after themselves, but the early training of the main stems is essential.

The floppier shrub roses, such as the centifolias, will also need some support, or the flowers will get muddy faces in wet weather. Again, obelisks are suitable, or, even less conspicuous, a frame of four wooden stakes to which you tie the main stems, just as you tie delphiniums to canes, but on a larger scale. One thick, rough stake will do, supplemented with a forked prop if necessary, a method used in the old rose garden at Kiftsgate.

What is the meaning in the rose catalogues of terms like 'semi-double' and 'very full'?

These terms refer to the petallage, and are explained in one of the Royal National Rose Society's booklets as follows:

A single rose has one row of five petals, though there may be two or three extra petals inside the main row. A semi-double rose has two to three complete rows of petals. A moderately full rose has fifteen to twenty-five petals, and a full rose twenty-six to forty petals. A very full rose has over forty petals.

CHAPTER X

Some Favourite Plants

Most of us worry too much about our gardens. I certainly do. Many gardeners, far from being gentle philosophers in tune with nature, are jumpy neurotics, and there is often nothing more anxiety-ridden than country cocktail party conversation. 'There were fifty perfect buds and then every one of the flowers fell off.' 'I think they're cut-worms but they could be flea-beetles.' 'We can't take a holiday this year because of the fruit.' 'The old fool used the wrong spray.'

Yet the point of a flower garden is pleasure. It is idiotic and unnecessary to let the garden become a tyrant and to be its self-appointed slave. For though the specialist gardeners may enjoy a nurse-patient relationship with tender and difficult plants, most of us prefer a give-and-take friendship; and for us, there are hundreds of consistently rewarding plants which rarely go wrong if they are given a little sensible treatment. I have been thinking about the plants in our own garden which have been consistently attractive and healthy, which I can recommend without reservation. I have divided them into four categories – Scented Flowers, White Flowers, Trouble-Free Plants and Exceptional Shrubs – and I have chosen ten of each which have served me particularly well.

Scented Flowers

I have a passion for scented flowers, which often means choosing an old-fashioned variety with more fragrance, but probably smaller flowers, than modern developments of the same flower.

Pre-Spencer Sweet Peas. A mixed packet of modern sweet peas will produce one of the highest rewards of the summer garden, a long succession of large sweet-smelling flowers for sniffing and cutting – as everybody knows, the more you cut, the more they grow. But it doubles the pleasures if you also grow a little separate row of the old pre-Spencer sweet peas (that is, sweet peas before Earl Spencer's head gardener bred the parent of all modern sweet peas in 1899). The flowers are smaller than those of modern sweet peas, not frilled, but very delicate in form and of an extraordinary fragrance. They are grown in Cranborne Manor and at Scotney Castle, where the walled cutting garden provides great baskets of flowers for the house. Neither seeds nor plants are easy to find, unless you are given some, as I was at Scotney by Mrs Christopher Hussey, but Messrs. Turral of Farnley, Otley, Yorks, who brought the old-fashioned sweet peas back into commerce, have an extensive list of plants. The oldest and most fragrant varieties are 'Matucana', a maroon and violet bi-colour, and 'Sicilian Pink', which is fuchsia pink and white. Unwin's have a selection of seeds.

Sweet Rocket. Sweet Rocket, or *Hesperis matronalis*, is a perfect border plant, growing some three feet high, covered with white or mauve scented flowers (often both on the same plant) for several weeks from the middle of May.

It is technically a perennial, but I find it better to take up all the plants after flowering except two, which will drop enough seeds to provide as many plants as are needed for the following year. The young plants flower better than the old woody ones, and as sweet rocket gets very bushy, one is glad of their space.

I have only the single form, but there are double forms of both white and mauve sweet rocket, the latter being rare, and I believe these have to be propagated by cuttings or division.

Scented-leaved geraniums. These are really foliage plants, for the flowers are insignificant, but the leaves make up for it. They come in various shapes and sizes, but all smell strongly if you pinch them, of lemon, orange, apple, spice, cedar or peppermint, as the case may be. I started with a collection of 'six all different' which I ordered at Chelsea from Greybridge Geraniums, of Evesham, and my husband took cuttings of the three we liked best and we now have a large stock. The three are *Pelargonium tomentosum*, a really lovely plant with large downy palmate leaves of fresh green deeply veined with dark green, and a peppermint smell; and two lemon-scented varieties, *P. graveolens* and a form of graveolens with variegated leaves called 'Lady Plymouth'. We leave them in the borders in summer and pot them up in October.

Jonquils. I am not an enthusiast for large trumpet daffodils, though of course I couldn't manage without a traditional piece of orchard with mixed daffodils naturalized in rough grass. But I love some of the smaller cyclamineus daffodils, especially 'March Sunshine', and some of the scented jonquils. The best of these is *Narcissus jonquilla* 'Trevithian', a tall jonquil with several butter-yellow flowers on each stem and a knockout scent. I have a pool of them in a poorish spot under elm trees, but they have done me proud, sending their scent to greet me whenever I plod in their direction. They deserve a better position.

Daphne odora 'Aureo-marginata'. It is hard to know which of the scented winter-flowering shrubs one likes best, and, if one decides on a daphne, then which of the many? I plump for this variety for a combination of perfection of flower, leaf and smell. *D. odora* needs a wigwam of bracken in winter in a cold garden, and though this margined variety is said to be less tender, it is certainly wise to protect it. If I lose mine one winter I shan't weep, for growing it is a calculated risk, but I shall put another in its place on the first good planting day. The one thing I will *not* do is protect it, as is sometimes advised, with a polythene bag. I would not subject so fine a plant to anything so unaesthetic.

Cottage Pinks. Dianthus of all sorts like my garden, but if I could have only one, though it would torture me to part with my sweet williams, I'd keep the cottage pinks. Their leaves are perfectly evergreen, or rather, ever-silver, and I find them more strongly scented than the hybrids. Except for Mrs Sinkins – I have her in both white and pink – I don't know the names of my pinks, nor where they came from; but mixed collections can be ordered from a few nurseries, notably from Allwood Brothers of Haywards Heath, who sell both plants and seeds, listing them delightfully as 'Fragrant Village Pinks'.

Iris Stylosa (unguicularis). Mr Bowles thought this the most indispensable plant in the garden and I'm not the person to contradict the great man. It produces surprisingly large lilac-mauve flowers feathered in yellow and white in the depths of winter which will fill your rooms with scent if you pick them in bud and bring them indoors. This iris asks for poor soil, good drainage and a place at the foot of a sunny wall.

Zéphirine Drouhin. It's invidious to choose just one from the many hundreds of scented roses, but if I had space for only one, it would be the Bourbon rose, Zéphirine Drouhin. It is not so highly scented as Etoile de Hollande, nor are the flowers of so soft a pink nor so well-shaped as the other great Bourbon, La Reine Victoria. But for a combination of scent, quantity of flower, good rosy foliage and general stamina, it's hard to beat. Our Zéphirine blooms from June well into October, and though the bush is old and very large, it still puts out strong new shoots from the ground every year.

Lily-of-the-Valley. A totally obvious choice, but that's no reason for not making it. Mine get a mulch of leaf-mould in the autumn, but are otherwise neglected, and they multiply like rabbits.

Lemon Thyme. I find *Thymus citriodorus*, an evergreen plant with the clean smell of lemons, the best of all small evergreen shrubs, but I have praised it in other chapters, and won't dilate again.

White Flowers

One of the nicest things about white flowers is the way they prolong the summer evenings. When it is almost dark, and the red and blue flowers and all the green leaves have sunk into shadow, one can walk round the garden and enjoy the ghostly, glimmering pools of white. Or one can sit indoors by an open window and look out on a scene which fades more slowly because white flowers are keeping the light alive. They have other qualities, too. They cool down colour schemes which might be garish, and many white flowers are scented.

Tobacco Plant. Tobacco plant has above all other plants this gift of prolonging the evening. Long after the lights are up and the curtains are drawn one can wander round the garden in the dark guided by their scent and whiteness. I buy a box of seedlings in the market every June and stuff them in wherever I can find a small space. They grow at a bursting pace, as though they'd eaten H. G. Wells's Food of the Gods, and flower all through August and September, or until the first frost. I like the red and lime green varieties, too, but the white are best. As plants from the market are somewhat haphazardly labelled, I never quite know how many I'm getting of each. A very tall and choice species for those with a greenhouse to start them off is *Nicotiana sylvestris*.

Galtonia candicans. Perhaps I wouldn't be so attached to this plant if I could grow better lilies, but for those on alkaline soil, galtonia makes a splendid lily substitute, sending up tall spikes of huge white bells which flower in August. They look happy among shrubs or in the border, and we have even tried a clump in the wild garden. I was furious when the old name, *Hyacinthus candicans*, went out of use, for it was more truly descriptive of the plant.

Philadelphus. I have yet to meet an unattractive philadelphus, whether single or double, open-flowered or cup-shaped. But some grow very thick and tall, which makes them difficult to prune, and I prefer the shorter, shrubbier ones, and the best of all is 'Belle Etoile'; it has flat white open flowers with a purple eye, and a scent which carries right across the garden. Few plants which are so hardy and easy have such a hothouse glamour as philadelphus. I trim mine religiously as soon as they have flowered, and they are massed with blossom every year.

Candytuft. The perennial candytuft, *Iberis sempervirens*, is whiter-than-white, as the commercials say, one of the few white flowers which does not look dirty beside snow. I love it among the

first yellows and greens of spring. I have planted it at the top of
a low wall and the evergreen mounds tumble over it to my great
gratitude, for the bricks are rather new and harsh. Often grown as
a rock or paving plant, it will make quite a big bush if left unclipped.
A common plant which is just too good to be 'ordinary'.

Crambe cordifolia. I met this ornamental sea-kale rather late in
my life, but have become a latter-day addict. It is grown in some of
my favourite gardens, like Cranborne Manor and Haseley Court,
and is a feature of the white border at Glyndebourne. It looks like
a giant gypsophila, growing some six feet high, with hundreds
of small white starry flowers growing in pannicles on branching
stalks. It is one of the largest and most splendid of all herbaceous
plants, and I can't think why I never encountered it sooner, as it
is fully hardy and likes limy soil.

Prunus subhirtella 'Autumnalis'. This prunus is a small tree
of pleasant shape, though most gardeners grow it primarily for
cutting. Branches or twigs brought into the house in winter will
open into pure white semi-double flowers which last for weeks,
and out-of doors it will flower on and off from November to
March if there is any mild, dry weather. I have a neighbour
with a handsome fourteen-year-old tree from which she cuts me
branches every Christmas time, but my own tree is still small,
alas, one year smaller than it need be, for the nursery sent me
a pink-flowered form by mistake. They readily changed it, but I
had lost a year's growth. The pink is a typical bright prunus pink,
cheap and cheerful, and the white, which is a true bridal white, is
much more beautiful.

Rose Iceberg. I don't usually grow impassioned about flowers which are top of the pops, but I'm an ardent member
of the Iceberg fan club. It may be common, but it is much
too good a flower ever to become vulgarized. It is a modern
floribunda with the real cabbage shape of old-fashioned roses
and a respectable amount of scent to add to its sterling virtues
of good health, abundance of flower and length of flowering
season. Sometimes it grows so large, even though pruned in
the spring, that it is clearly pretending to be a shrub rose,

but unlike most shrub roses, it flowers on and on. A great modern rose.

Solomon's Seal. Years ago, I knew a damp wood which was full of this lovely plant growing wild, but the wood was bulldozed long ago and I have found none in our neighbourhood since. Now I have it in the garden, a healthy drift of *Polygonatum multiflorum* under a large cotoneaster, where it holds its own in a struggle for existence with naturalized *Helleborus viridis*, campanulas and columbines. It is a very subtle plant, with its arched stems hung with white bells tinged with green. I give it leaf-mould in late autumn, though I think that the cotoneaster leaves, when they fall, would probably provide enough mulch.

White Tulips. I have gone through many tulip phases – Darwins, parrots, cottage tulips and tulip species have all attracted me in turn – and am currently devoted to the tulips with pointed petals called lily-flowered. (The trouble with parrot tulips is that their fascinating frilly heads are too heavy for their bodies, and the stalks are apt to snap while the tulips are at their peak.)

Of the lily-flowered tulips, I would pin-point 'White Triumphator' as a superb variety; I always plant it with the crimson 'Captain Fryatt' which is also, if it is not libellous to some gallant officer to say so, lily-flowered. I sometimes plant them in alternate groups, and sometimes mix them together. I am very extravagant with tulips and buy new ones every year. Lifting them, burying them over a piece of wire netting in a trench until the leaves die down, and then storing them is an appalling labour, and the only time I did it the bulbs in their trench were chewed to bits by slugs. This has never happened to me with tulips left in the ground, and I think lifting and storing is a routine for professional gardeners rather than busy amateurs.

Gypsophila. I don't grow many annuals, for they tend to add to the spottiness of a garden which already contains too many different plants. But every spring we scatter seeds of the half-hardy annual *Gypsophila elegans* in the main border, choosing places which we think may look a bit skimpy in July. Being a very branching plant, it fills the spaces perfectly, and we enjoy the tremulous white starry flowers for weeks, both in the garden and cut for the house.

Trouble-Free Plants

The plants which are so reliable and loyal that one wants to thank them every year one sees them are not the same for every gardener. In my case, the faithful band are all lime-lovers, but in another garden, they may all be marsh plants. However, I think most of the ten I have chosen will grow anywhere. They are plants which look after themselves. You do next to nothing for them, but every year, they put on their best dress.

Alchemilla mollis. I have mentioned this plant many times and will not describe it again, but will just dwell for a moment on its virtues. It is graceful in flower and leaf, it flowers for a long period, it makes weed-proof ground cover, it makes cushions in the border, it will grow in sun or shade and is perfect for cutting. If that isn't recommendation enough, you are hard to please. Its vices, I think, are nil.

Campanula persicifolia. I adore all campanulas. Even the grandest forms have a wild, Ophelia quality which I like. But *C. persicifolia* is my choice because it naturalizes well, seeds all over the garden, but is easy to control, as its roots are spreading and shallow, *and it doesn't need staking*. How I hate staking! I don't grow the tall beautiful pink campanula 'Loddon Anna' because I can't face the job of keeping her upright. At Scotney, she is grown in such tight company with shrubs that she doesn't need staking, but when I grew her for a time she always found a way of falling on her face. *C. persicifolia*, both mauve and white forms, flowers on and off from June to October. It is not, I must admit, very good for cutting.

Japanese Anemone. This is what you and I call *Anemone japonica*, but I shall avoid the Latin name, as I conclude from much studying of dictionaries that it ought to be called *A. hupehensis* or possibly *A. elegans*, or possibly something quite different, like *Anemone × elegans* var. 'Japonica' × *hupeensis* cv. *Bowlesii-Stearnii*. Anyway, the Japanese anemone is another dear good plant which needs no staking. This lovely thing grows to at least 4 feet in my garden. The stems are upright and strong and the flowers which look so fragile are as tough as old boots, flower from late August right into October and provide fresh, springlike bouquets for the house when all else is berries and 'autumn tints'. Even the smaller buds come out in water. The vine-like leaves are bright and glossy. All this obliging plant needs is dividing from time to time, as it is a great spreader, but otherwise, a blob of manure in spring is its only request.

Loosestrife. The best weed suppressor I know is the yellow loose-strife, *Lysimachia punctata*, the best possible plant for filling newly reclaimed ground. If you have a piece of weedy ground, get the weeds out and put in yellow loosestrife at once – even the nettles will have to acknowledge defeat. It spreads rapidly and is happy in sun or shade. I have a large clump of it in an excessively shady spot which becomes quite bright and cheerful when the whorls of yellow flowers are out.

Pulmonaria. One of the prettiest of all spring flowers, pulmonaria, or lungwort, 'Soldiers and Sailors' or 'Joseph and Mary', not only produces pink-and-blue flowers in April but large decorative spotted leaves almost all the year round. These leaves are good in vases in late autumn with any odd flowers which may be going. It is a good ground cover plant, harmonizing well, I find, with roses, and spreads fast. Pulmonaria prefers a damp corner, but is not insistent, and mine do well in various parts of the garden; but I do see that taller plants give them a little protection from the hottest summer sun.

Rose Maigold. All roses give trouble. They get blackspot, or they sucker, or they scratch you when you prune them, or they demand extra feeds, or they grow over the roof and stop up the gutters, or they think up some other way of annoying you. But Maigold is the nearest thing to a trouble-free rose I've found except for the rose species. It grows to a convenient height, and I, who am tall, can just reach the top branches from a kitchen chair – I have an aversion to ladders. It flowers prodigiously once a year without fail, in late May or early June, and makes a creditable second effort in late summer. The pruning is easy – I just saw off one thick old stem at the base every autumn – and I give Maigold one annual mulch of manure at the same time. This is certainly a rose for the busy.

Euphorbia: 1. We have at least twenty different euphorbias in the garden, but not all are trouble-free. For instance, the noble *E. wulfenii* is far from hardy. But *E. griffithii* 'Fireglow' is a first-rate plant, with brilliant flame-coloured flowers (technically called bracts) which glow for most of the summer. Grow it in sunshine, or they won't glow.

Euphorbia: 2. *E. epithymoides* is almost as important to me as alchemilla and it has some of the same good qualities: a round, cushiony shape, perfect health and a capacity for blanketing all weeds. The sulphur-yellow flowers are very striking in late April and May, but the plant gets rather large and heavy after flowering; I usually cut down the outer stalks.

So inordinately fond am I of this plant that one spring we found the entire garden was spotted with blinding clumps of yellow – one unkind visitor put on sun-glasses to protect her eyes. I was persuaded to remove some clumps altogether and to rearrange the others into just a few groups.

Ivy. Having a mass of old ivy in my hedges and under the trees, it was only lately that I thought of planting decorative ivies; the idea came to me after admiring them at several R.H.S. flower shows. I assumed, mistakenly, that they would race over walls and cover drainpipes in a season, but far from it, they are slow starters, barely moving in their first year. But once started, I think the ivies, all of which are hardy, are among the most attractive and useful of all climbing plants. I now have two variegated ivies climbing well, both evergreen and both self-clinging. The more charming is *Hedera helix* 'Goldheart', with small brilliant green leaves with bright yellow centres. The most useful is *H. canariensis*, with large pale yellow leaves with a grey-green variegation. Having got going at last, it is doing its required job of masking a drainpipe very efficiently. It is alleged to be tender, but it seems hardy to me. The variegated ivies need some sunshine or they won't variegate; for deep shade, all-green varieties must be chosen. A great advantage of green ivy is that it is the one plant which mixes well with daffodils in a bowl, daffodils being, to my mind, a stiff flower in the house, and far from easy to arrange.

Crocus tomasinianus. I have bad crocus trouble in my garden because I am the unwilling hostess to hundreds of sparrows and mice. The sparrows dust-bath in the beds in summer and scratch up the bulbs and the mice eat them. To survive, my crocuses have to be naturalized in grass, and, though most do well in this fashion, the species *C. tomasinianus* is the best of all, flowering very early and spreading rapidly. I have mixed the usual lilac colour with a darker variety called 'Whitewell Purple', which I bought from Broadleigh Nurseries, and the two blues together make quite a happy splash.

Exceptional Shrubs

By 'exceptional shrubs' I mean 'exceptionally good shrubs' rather than rare ones, and an exceptionally good shrub, by my standards, has to be perfectly hardy, must have a beautiful shape, and must have some peculiar interest of its own, whether of leaf, flower, berry or bark – what is in Fleet Street called a 'talking point'. And it must look as though it enjoys life in my garden, for I do not like reluctant guests.

Cornus alba 'Elegantissima'. I have no doubts about my choice of the best shrub of all. It is that supreme dogwood, *Cornus alba* 'Elegantissima', which seems to me to have no fault. It grows into a graceful thicket, and the soft green leaves margined with white stay fresh all summer through; in autumn they drop off quickly and neatly to reveal the red polished stems which are one of the delights of winter. This dogwood has to be pruned hard in spring, as the red wood is the young wood; like most shrubs, it may need watering for its first summer or two until well established.

Cotoneaster 'Rothschildianus'. You remember the donkey which hesitated for so long between two bales of straw that in the end it starved to death? I was like this for years about the two exciting, but very similar cotoneasters, C. 'Exburiensis' and C. 'Rothschildianus', not knowing which was the better nor which to order. Both produce huge clusters of rich yellow berries in autumn, both grow in an arching shape, and have pointed, willow-like leaves which are nearly evergreen. Then I read Mr Russell Page's *Education of a Gardener*, in which he names C. 'Rothschildianus' as the finest of all cotoneasters. This decided me, and I planted one as a specimen shrub in rough grass in a conspicuous position just to one side of what is laughingly called our main axis. I am delighted that I did so. It produced some of the luscious berries in the first autumn after planting and is shooting strongly into a handsome shape.

A Purple Nut. Nut-trees grow very well in our part of the world, and we usually have more hazels, cobs and filberts than we can dispose of. They are ideal shelter plants, and as we had space for another, I thought it worth trying a decorative nut. *Corylus maxima* 'Purpurea', so long as it is planted in sunshine, has glorious purple leaves and seems quite as sturdy as the others. I think this is the variety grown in the red and purple garden at Hidcote.

Mahonia 'Charity'. Mahonias are not everybody's meat, for they are spiky and awkward. In the summer, I grudge the space my *Mahonia japonica* takes up, but when I cut the scented yellow flowers in winter, I reproach myself. *M.* 'Charity' grows vertically, not bushily, into a tall prickly spike sprouting with vertical sprays of flower, and I am inclined to think it the better of the two. It has a Gothic look and I am sure Ruskin would have liked it. It is quite a fast grower, needs some shade and perhaps a bit of underplanting in maturity, if the tall bare stalk offends you. I see it essentially as a specimen shrub, but my nearest shrub nursery, Sherrard's of Newbury, took a single order one year for 32 plants. I long to find out how they were planted.

Winter Jasmine. I have mentioned *Jasminum nudiflorum* in earlier chapters and every gardener knows it, the greatest of all shrubs for north walls, heavy shade or indifferent soil. I never grow tired of it, and from December on am never short of cut flowers, for I pick the branches in bud and bring them into the house where they open into sprays of yellow stars.

Kolkwitzia amabilis. I am surprised that more gardeners do not grow this beautiful shrub, for I find it more graceful, both in shape and flower, than its near relation, the weigela. It quickly grows into a light thicket, with the outer branches spraying out like a fountain, and is covered every June with small pink bell-flowers with yellow throats. It is admirably hardy, and the leaves turn pleasantly crimson in autumn.

Spiraea arguta. Another shrub which grows like a fountain, and one of the earliest to flower, is *Spiraea arguta*, the 'Bridal Wreath'. Every spray is laden with tiny white flowers in April. I find it grows taller than the catalogues tell you, and as it increases with several new shoots from the ground every year, it needs plenty of space. Mine are too cramped – I underestimated their ultimate size.

Viburnum tomentosum 'Mariesii'. I wish I had space for fifty different viburnums, for *V. carlesii* and *V. davidii* and *V. burkwoodii* and many more. As it is, I have only four varieties, all deserving a heartfelt testimonial, but this variety, with its flat branches of white lace-cap flowers, is the best of all. I have described it fully in a previous chapter, so will not plug 'Mariesii' again.

Elaeagnus pungens 'Maculata'. This is the most brilliantly cheerful of all winter plants. It doesn't offer a sweet smell, or shy little early flowers, or other delicate gifts. It is just a great blob of bright green and gold in winter. It is a slow-growing variety, but strong and hardy, and of a fine bushy shape.

Genista lydia. This is one of my favourite dwarf shrubs, a charming little weeping broom covered with bright yellow flowers in May and June. Few brooms are happy in my garden, but this miniature member of the family has taken kindly to a rough, dry bank and is one of the greatest pleasures of early summer.

CHAPTER XI

Gardening on Chalk or Lime

I must have had a presentiment when young that I would one day live on the Berkshire downs, for at a very early age, I took a dislike to rhododendrons. Perhaps I was hit on the head with a rhododendron in my pram, or had some unfortunate experience in a shrubbery in my formative years; whatever the reason, I have never, when praising the exquisite rhododendrons and azaleas of my friends, managed to sound quite sincere.

It is therefore no pain to me that my garden is on chalk. If I ever move (which is unlikely) I would seek a more sheltered spot, where I could grow more tender things than I can manage now, or perhaps a garden with a stream, for I would dearly love to try my hand with marsh plants, but I would not seek an acid soil. Chalk is not all toil and trouble – it drains well and is easier to work than heavy clay – and is the natural home of thousands of charming plants. The very limitations of a chalk garden are a stimulus. You become a bit of a specialist, learning to sift the calcicoles from the calcifuges and feeling profound satisfaction every time you discover a new lime-lover.

About seven per cent of the British Isles is on chalk, mostly, though not exclusively, in the south of England, so that chalk gardening might seem a minority subject. But there are other less extreme forms of alkaline soil – either limestone or marl – in parts of nearly every county in England, from Cornwall to Northumberland. Probably one-sixth of Britain's gardeners are working on limy soil – that is, with a *p*H reaction higher than 7 – and they face two particular problems.

First, they are limited in their choice of plants, for though most plants will grow on an acid soil, many utterly refuse to grow on an alkaline soil. And secondly, they usually have to enrich the soil itself. In the case of chalk, the soil is often thin and is always quick-draining, and for both reasons, needs constant enrichment.

Choosing plants for chalk is fascinating, and anyone gardening on chalk for the first time should start by doing a bit of reading, a bit of motoring and a bit of walking.

He should start by reading the late Sir Frederick's Stern's *A Chalk Garden* at least three times, and by the third reading he will have been fired with a great love of chalk and will realize that anyone messing about with rhododendrons and Japanese maples is wasting his time.

He should then get out his car (assuming it's summer) and go and visit the garden at Highdown, in Sussex, which is the subject of Sir Frederick's book. Sir Frederick started to make this great garden in 1909, and he made it in a disused chalk-pit, starting at a time when the available knowledge of lime-loving plants was scanty and most of the experimental work was still to be done. Many of the great botanical expeditions to North and West China, which produced so many lime-loving plants, had not yet set forth – Sir Frederick later contributed to expeditions by Reginald Farrer and Frank Kingdon Ward – and the seeds and cuttings of plants which we all grow now were then the rare treasures of connoisseurs. Today, Highdown is a paradise as bountiful as any garden on rich woodland soil, but all the plants are lime-lovers. Snowdrops, daffodils, anemones, paeonies, tulips, flowering cherries, irises, hellebores and eremurus are Highdown specialities, and the more curious plants include the charming handkerchief-tree, *Davidia involucrata*, discovered in China by the French missionary, Père David, and *Echium scilloniensis*, a spiky obelisk of a plant from Tresco, in the Scilly Isles.

If Highdown is not on your beat, there are many other famous gardens on chalk or lime which are open to the public; for instance, Charleston Manor, in Sussex, Polesden Lacey, in Surrey, Wilton House, in Wiltshire, and Cranborne Manor, in Dorset, all on chalk, and Hidcote Manor and Kiftsgate Court, both in Gloucestershire, and Haseley Court in Oxfordshire, all three on lime. Two outstanding limy gardens in the north of England are at Snape Castle, in the North Riding, and Harrington Hall, in Lincolnshire.

A third way of learning about chalk-loving plants is to do a bit of walking in chalk country, to see what grows wild. The wild clematis is so rampant in my district that it gives a quick clue to the fact that clematis are insatiable for lime. The wild hellebore in our local woods, *Helleborus viridis*, leads one on to the whole family of hellebores, and the Pasque flower, *Anemone pulsatilla*, on the local downs, to the family of anemones, and the soapwort which flourishes on the village waste ground to the dianthus family. The exuberance of our local bluebells and the survival, only fifty miles from London, of wild daffodils and snowdrops, show that most bulbs love chalk, and the dogwoods, yews and spindles on the downs are pointers to chalk-loving shrubs. There is great pleasure in working this sort of thing out for yourself.

I am sure that the first principle for chalk gardeners is to grow what is natural for their site. It is possible, and it's sometimes done in our district, to make special peat beds for azaleas, but I think they have a cheap theatrical look in a bare downland landscape. It is as though somebody had painted the elms out of a Gainsborough landscape and painted in palm-trees instead. There are so many plants which thrive on chalk that I do not see the point of the struggle.

If you have a passion for some lime-hating plant, grow it in tubs or pots or in a peat-filled sink or trough, so that it is clearly a 'specimen' plant, a visitor from another climate. If you try to make it blend with the natural flora in the open ground, it will look as phoney as those colourful beds of growing plants at a flower show.

Plants for the chalk garden divide into three classes:

The ardent chalk lovers.

The plants which usually tolerate lime.

The mixed families of plants, like the lily family, of which some will tolerate lime and others won't.

As a rule-of-thumb, plants which originate from the Mediterranean, where many of the formations are limestone, and from China, do well on chalk, while those from North America and Japan, with a different geological structure, require more acid soil; but this is a rough rule with many exceptions, and some plants are native to both China and Japan.

The Ardent Chalk-Lovers

Five families of plants should have their names inscribed on a chalk-lovers' Roll of Honour, hellebores, clematis, paeonies, cyclamen and dianthus.

In praising hellebores, it is impossible to lay it on too thick. They are superb plants. They have natural grace of form, elegant bell-shaped flowers, and beautiful deep-cut foliage, which is evergreen in most varieties; yet they are hardy and reliable, flowering in the worst months of the year when even the early bulbs prefer to stay underground. *H. corsicus* is the most spectacular, growing in rotund bushes two feet high; the proud clusters of huge pale green bells sometimes begin to flower in mid-winter, when one is frantic for excitement. (So heavy are the heads that they may need to be propped up with pea-sticks.) *H. orientalis*, the Lenten rose, is the most varied in colour, for the bells may be white, pinkish, greenish or plum colour, and the shades will change as the flowers develop. *H. foetidus*, which grows wild all over France, from Normandy to the Dordogne, has smaller bells than *H. corsicus*, but dozens of them on every plant, and it is impervious to bad weather. The evergreen leaves never have a bad moment. *H. viridis*, which grows wild near my cottage, is a modest little plant, for the flowers are of exactly the same green as the rich, deep-cut leaves, and so are not conspicuous, but if you look closely, you find that the small, delicate bells have the same fragile beauty as a harebell. This hellebore is not evergreen, but vanishes in summer, the leaves unfurling from the ground in early spring like bracken. Gardeners have different views as to the flowering order of the hellebores. In my garden, *H. corsicus* is the first to form visible buds, sometimes about Christmas, but the date on which they open depends entirely on the weather.

Clematis are made for the chalk gardener, for they don't just tolerate lime, they insist on it, and your friend with a peaty soil will never grow such fine flowers as yours.

Every clematis gardener knows that you have to feed well, water well and shade the roots, but there is a further complication which has only lately entered my consciousness, that you must select your varieties carefully for sun or shade.

My own Nelly Moser is in a sunny corner, and though it flowers profusely, the lilac stripes soon fade, while my *C. orientalis*, on the other hand, is in too shady a spot to flower as freely as it should. I am beginning to think that most clematis would rather have too little sun than too much, especially the large-flowered hybrids, and many will grow on a north wall. But some of the later clematis, like *C. orientalis* and *C. tangutica*, seem to want to nod their small yellow lantern heads in full sun.

Clematis are the most difficult of flowers to write about, for the descriptions of many quite different varieties sound exactly the same; search as you may for the right descriptive adjective, you can only come up with 'large mauve-blue sepals' or 'handsome purple-blue flowers'. Every gardener must choose his clematis for himself, and luckily they lend themselves perfectly to exhibition and are usually among the best displays at flower shows. If I had to limit myself to three, I would choose *C. macropetala* for early flowering – it has inky buds which open into nodding mauve-blue semi-double flowers, and very delicate foliage. It is essentially a scrambler, and likes to wander through a shrub or short, bushy tree.

For the midsummer period, I would choose 'Mrs Cholmondeley', with huge light blue flowers which go on for weeks. For late summer, I would have *C. viticella* 'Alba Luxurians', with white flowers delightfully tipped with green. I first saw this uncommon clematis in Mrs Fish's garden, so of course I had to have it, though I had to wait a year before I could find a nursery with any stock.

Paeonies are another family which thrives in the chalk garden – nearly all wild paeonies grow on limestone, many of them in China – but their flowering season, though delicious, is short, and I think they are best grown in masses in a large garden; in a small garden they can take up more space than they earn. Though lovely when the leaves are young and when in full flower, their manner of dying is somewhat sordid, and they take a long time about it. For this reason, I am trying to banish all large paeonies to the wild garden, and to have only that lovely dwarf paeony, *P. officinalis* 'Anemoneflora', in the border, where the delphiniums can cover it after flowering. This paeony has satiny crimson flowers and a bluish bloom on the leaves, and I cannot think why it is so rarely grown.

The big fat paeonies which I have moved to the wild garden seem to be settling down, especially the red cottage paeonies and a rich double pink affair which I think is 'Lady Alexandra Duff'. The tree paeonies, *P. lutea ludlowii*, look less happy, but they must learn to like their wild life, for I won't have this paeony in domestic quarters. It spends three months in the autumn dying down, shedding leaves and stalks disgustingly – the red amputated limbs are pure Hieronymus Bosch – and I am not enamoured of the bare sticks which remain through the winter.

All the cyclamen can be counted among the ardent lime-lovers. Anyone who has seen them in the limestone mountains of Greece, nestling in the ancient ruins and forming pink pools between grey stones, will know that they are a natural for the limy garden. I believe it is possible, by careful selection of varieties, to have cyclamen in flower nearly all the year round; but there are so many charming small flowers in spring, and so few in autumn and winter, that the late varieties, like C. *neapolitanum*, are the ones I want to establish. My enemy is the birds, which scratch up the corms and peck the flowers before they have seeded, so I am getting small colonies going under thick, low shrubs, and hope the birds won't notice them.

Dianthus also do well in a chalk garden, liking the drainage and the lime. I find that old-fashioned cottage pinks and sweet williams do amazingly well in my garden. Both need to be planted in ground which has been enriched with some well rotted manure or compost and with bonemeal, and the pinks must be kept well-clipped so that they form cushions.

The hardy hybrids are more difficult, and I wouldn't recommend them to the gardener who is too busy for the finicky extra attention they require. On the other hand, they flower for a longer period than the cottage pinks, though the scent is not so intense. They are supposed to need hoof-and-horn dug in before planting, a thinning of the shoots in spring, and liquid feeds in spring and summer; they get the hoof-and-horn from me, but not the after-care, and results are middling.

Though I have given a medal of honour to these five families, many other plants are wholly reliable on chalk, provided each gets the sort of cultivation it needs.

Euphorbias in great variety, hardy geraniums, campanulas, from the smallest rock campanulas to giant Canterbury Bells, anemones, helianthemums, monarda, oriental poppies, the borage family, most bulbs and annuals, especially nigella, gypsophila and nicotiana, asters, heleniums, scabious, penstemons, many saxifrages, sweet-rocket, foxgloves, columbines, hostas, doronicum, loosestrife, angelica and all things umbelliferous, woody herbs like sage and lavender, echinops, sunflowers, alchemilla, honeysuckle, vines, crambe, acanthus, stocks, nepeta, wallflowers, periwinkles, iberis (both annual and perennial), valerian, achillea, antirrhinums, galega, bocconias, petunias, dahlias, lily-of-the-valley, primroses, polyanthus and sedum have all grown contentedly in my garden, and better gardeners than I could treble this list. Those with more sheltered gardens than mine can grow one of the most perfect plants in the world, *Romneya coulteri*, the Californian Tree Poppy, which delights in lime. This lovely giraffe grows seven or eight feet tall, and has large white scented flowers with papery petals which flutter like a dancer's tutu.

Possibly irises should take a front seat among the chalk lovers, but I am not sure. Certainly all the well-known irises except *I. kaempferi* and *I. laevigata* enjoy lime and good drainage, but my own results with the tall bearded irises have been adequate rather than exciting. I find they are not good mixers in the border and I haven't room for a special iris bed. But I have done well with some intermediate bearded irises, about twelve inches high, which I planted a few years ago, and which harmonize well with herbaceous plants or shrubs.

Coming to shrubs, the catalogue of lime-lovers is infinite. I believe the majority of shrubs tolerate lime, and though one must forgo rhododendrons, azaleas, camellias, hamamelis, tree heathers, vaccinium, pieris and Japanese maples, one can stuff the garden with dogwoods, whitebeam, cistuses, buddleias, potentillas, elaeagnus, euonymus, santolina, lilac, jasmine, *Osmanthus delavayi*, hypericum, senecio, some veronicas, most prunus, berberis, kolkwitzia, weigela, spiraea, viburnums in all their great variety, cotoneaster, philadelphus, daphne, yew and box, and, luckily, with all the fragrant winter-flowering shrubs except *Hamamelis mollis. Viburnum fragrans*, *Mahonia japonica*, *M.* 'Charity' and *Chimonanthus praecox* revel in lime. The deepest deprivation one suffers is the camellia, and if I were ever tempted to betray my philosophy and make a peat bed, it would be to grow a pink and white striped camellia.

The gardener who, through shortage of time, space or inclination, doesn't want to experiment and risk failure, could have a thickly populated garden by choosing well-known lime-lovers such as these.

Plants Which Usually Tolerate Lime

There are a number of plants which are willing to put up with lime, *so long as the other factors are in their favour.* One cannot be dogmatic about them. They may hit, they may miss. One of these plants may thrive in your neighbour's garden and refuse to put out a leaf in yours, though he has kindly handed some plants in prime condition over the garden fence.

These chancy plants are interesting to grow, but to have any success, you must know your garden well. The professionals call it 'knowing your micro-climate'. You need to know not only where the soil is least limy, but also where the drainage is best and the topsoil deepest, for often a calcifuge will do well if the soil is rich and full of good food.

How far you are willing to experiment depends on your attitude to growing difficult things, which depends in turn on how much time and money you can spare. My own creed is never to go beyond three successive failures with any variety (or two failures in the case of an expensive shrub) because I can't bear forcing plants to eke out a miserable existence feeling ill. I try them in different parts of the garden, try the merits of a bit more food, and occasionally a dose of Sequestrene, which provides iron for chlorosis patients. Then, if they still look sickly, euthanasia is the thing.

Here are my own experiences with some of the hit-or-miss plants.

Sweet peas grow extremely well for me, in the best part of the garden. They are supposed to be vulnerable to striation, or 'striping', in lime soils, but I have not found it so. The only year they failed in my garden was when I was away during a drought and they never got watered, and they wilted, not from lime, but from thirst.

Phlox, like sweet peas, will grow on a chalk soil if they get enough food and drink. I doubt if they ever attain their fullest size on lime, but the delicious scent is undiminished, a sweet compensation for the dusty boredom of August.

Lupins are notorious lime-haters – on chalk, the leaves soon go yellow and die back – but I have one clump of pink lupins in a shady corner which is reminder that one must never lay down the law in gardening. It flowers profusely year after year and the foliage remains a good strong green. I have tested the soil where they grow and the lime content is *p*H8, so why do they flourish? It must be the depth of topsoil, which is a good three feet.

Other chancy plants are the brooms, which some chalk gardeners can grow while others can't – I fail with all the cytisus group and with most genistas except the charming weeping dwarf broom, *Genista lydia*. Some can grow magnolias while others fail with the same varieties, even with the scented, lime-tolerant *M. stellata*. I fail with this, but I think the trouble is the strong winds in my garden, for I ran out of sheltered corners long ago. It's a case of one of the 'other factors', food, shelter, or moisture, being wrong for the plant.

Some can grow the lovely blue poppy, *Meconopsis betonicifolia*, though many can't, but this is such a beautiful plant that it is worth trying and taking trouble. Some succeed with difficult primulas, while others fail with such simple plants as elaeagnus or philadelphus or even (astonishing to me), with the lime-loving paeony. I am told that some chalk gardeners cannot grow monarda (bergamot) or Japanese anemones, but in my garden both spread like weeds. On the other hand, I cannot grow the miniature hoop-petticoat daffodil, nor the common almond tree, nor dictamnus, the Burning Bush plant, nor that charming cottage plant, *Dicentra spectabilis*, which annoyingly makes huge clumps in another garden in the village. As for the winter aconite, it is time somebody stood up and denounced the plant, which many writers say 'will grow anywhere', lying in their teeth. I cannot establish winter aconites in a single corner of my garden, and have decided that they are too temperamental to persevere with.

Fruit growing is outside the scope of this book, but I find that though many fruit trees and bushes do well, they have to be carefully selected, especially apples. Cox's, alas, are not at their best on chalk, but Charles Ross, which is a good eater and Bramley's Seedling, which is the best cooker in the world, both do splendidly, and crab apples thrive. As fruit trees are expensive and slow, one should consult a really good grower before ordering. It is barmy to plant trees which you have picked up casually without getting advice first.

Another quirk of the chalk garden is that you have to grow some perennial plants as biennials. This is true of the verbascums. I have a passion for the primrose yellow *V.* 'Gainsborough', but have to replant every year. And Iceland poppies have a way of vanishing. These are sometimes listed as 'perennials, best grown as biennials', which seems a slightly impertinent way of putting it. Nor do 'silver' plants, like the helichrysums, last more than a year with me; I try to remember to take cuttings, but usually forget and have to buy more. However, the silvery artemisias are more accommodating.

As a philosophy, I think it's worth giving mildly calcifuge plants a trial, provided the struggle is not stubbornly prolonged. But hopelessly calcifuge plants, like camellias, rhododendrons, azaleas, vacciniums, kalmia, hamamelis and Japanese maples will only be a disappointment.

The Mixed Families

There are certain families of plants which are hopelessly divided in their views on lime. Some members of the family like lime, others don't. Roses and lilies are prominent among these families, and heathers, magnolias, hydrangeas and primulas are others with mixed tastes.

Since roses are expensive and take time to give their best results, most gardeners would prefer to have some foreknowledge of the varieties which are likely to suit them, rather than to carry out their own experiments. I learned the hard way myself, and over the years have discarded many roses which were not prolific. The roses I am left with are beautiful and strong.

I will start with the sweeping statement that hybrid tea roses should not be grown on chalk. With deep digging before planting and plenty of good food, the stronger hybrid teas, like Shot Silk, Betty Uprichard, Madame Butterfly or Ena Harkness, will do tolerably well, but will not produce a full quota of flowers, while weaker hybrid teas are sure to develop chlorosis, a yellowing disease, in the second year. However, this warning applies *only to chalk*, not to a rich lime-and-clay soil, which suits many roses well.

Having choked you off hybrid teas, I would also like to discourage you from putting too much effort into miniature roses and the old-fashioned Provence roses, especially the moss section. But after that, all is good cheer.

Nearly all floribunda roses, nearly all climbing roses and a very large number of shrub roses, both old-fashioned and modern, will do extremely well. The cottages in our district are as thickly covered with roses in June as the cottages in Essex or Somerset, and many local gardens have rose hedges, groups of old-fashioned roses in the lawn, and roses to cut for the house from May to October.

I would say that you are safe with almost any good floribunda rose. Queen Elizabeth, the incomparable Iceberg, Plentiful, with pink, cupshaped flowers like a Bourbon rose, the nearly perpetual, quartered red Rosemary Rose and its scarlet offspring, Europeana, are a few of the many floribundas which grow as well on chalk as anywhere else. I always find yellow roses difficult, but Allgold and Chinatown are among the more reliable.

Climbing roses are highly satisfactory, and many climbing varieties of famous hybrid teas will give you a hybrid tea type of flower if you want it. Climbing Etoile de Hollande, Climbing Lady Hillingdon, Climbing Madame Butterfly and Climbing Caroline Testout have all done well in my garden, though the first did not live to a great age. Chalk usually means a shorter life for roses.

Other climbers and ramblers which I have seen grown on chalk with great success are Albertine, New Dawn, Dr van Fleet, Bobbie James, Guinée, Madame Alfred Carrière, Madame Gregoire Staechelin, Paul's Lemon Pillar, Souvenir de Claudius Denoyel, Zéphirine Drouhin, Sander's White, Albéric Barbier and Wedding Day. The yellow climbers may present some difficulty, particularly the pretty, small-flowered *Rosa foetida* 'Persiana', which hates lime and should not be attempted. But Mermaid is an outstanding exception, a superb rose for any soil.

Shrub roses are a marvellously interesting group of flowers, and anyone who cares for them should read *The Old Shrub Roses*, by Graham Stuart Thomas, who traces their lineage and charts the characteristics of each branch of the family with scholarly precision, until you feel you are a personal friend of the Bourbon and damask roses, the Old Moss Roses and the musks.

Mr Thomas is not primarily concerned in this book with problems of soil and cultivation, but I know from experience and observation that many of the old shrub roses grow well on chalk, with the possible exception of the Provence roses. I think the centifolias can be successful – I am watching an Old Cabbage Rose newly planted in my own garden, and a Fantin-Latour in a neighbour's garden with deep interest – but the moss roses are bad candidates for quick-draining soil. The modern shrub roses which have been developed from the old ones are nearly all successful on chalk, and as, for the practical gardener, there is no need to distinguish between the old and the new, I will mix them all up together. The best modern ones have the same old-fashioned beauty of bloom, the same wild type of foliage, and the same scent.

The hybrid musks are splendid on chalk, like the apricot Buff Beauty, the double white Prosperity and deep mauve Magenta, all richly scented with a spicy musk smell. If you want to see hybrid musks growing with wild profusion in a chalk garden, try to visit Cranborne Manor, in Dorset, on an 'open' day. This large Elizabethan garden specializes in scented flowers of every kind.

All the rugosa roses do well. Several gardening writers, and very good ones, too, have questioned this, but I can find no evidence for their distrust. In each case, the writers are gardeners on acid soil and I think are unduly suspicious. The only difficulty I have found with rugosas is that they may need watering in a drought.

I have found that *Rosa rugosa* (the type) spreads almost too eagerly, its roots running horizontally not far below the surface and sending up another shoot about two feet away, which can be inconvenient if the chosen spot for its arrival happens to be in the middle of a clump of paeonies.

R. rugosa Sarah van Fleet is the perfect rose for a hedge, with bright green deeply veined foliage and pink, semi-double flowers of luscious old-fashioned shape which recur through the summer after the first June flush. *R. rugosa* Frau Dagmar Hastrup, with soft pink single flowers and the best hips in the business, does well. So does *R.*

rugosa Blanc Double de Coubert, with papery flowers, the best of all white roses in my eyes. *R. rugosa* Mrs Anthony Waterer is a fine dark red scented rose, and *R. rugosa* Pink Grootendorst has crowded clusters of small pink flowers, pretty little frilled things like cottage pinks. These are some of the rugosas which I have grown myself, and I have pompously repeated the words *R. rugosa* every time by way of thumbing my nose at superior persons growing roses on acid soil who doubt that chalk people can grow rugosas.

Nearly all the rose species, of which so many come from China, and their direct hybrids, like chalk. There are *R. moyesii* (small scarlet flowers, like the flowers of a wild rose, smothering the bush in June); *R. rubrifolia* (exquisite sprays of blue-green leaves backed with scarlet); *R. xanthina* Canary Bird (fern-like leaves and long stems crowded with small yellow flowers in May); *R. farreri persetosa*, the Threepenny Bit rose; *R. cantabrigiensis* (creamy flowers in May and black hips later); *R. willmottiae*, a very tall rose species with lilac flowers; and the superb giant climbing species rose from China, *R. filipes*, which will smother a house or a tree with its heavy trusses of white scented flowers.

The hybrid perpetuals are satisfactory, though they are not much grown today; yet the pure white Frau Karl Druschki is a great rose. So are the damask roses (if well fed), like the clear pink Ispahan and the incomparable Madame Hardy, a white quartered rose with a green eye. So are most of the Bourbon roses, notably La Reine Victoria, with fold upon fold of fragrant mauve-pink petals cupped into a heavy blossom. But Variegata di Bologna is an exception, falling an easy victim in chalky soil to blackspot or chlorosis.

There are so many superb modern shrub roses that every gardener should visit nurseries or private gardens in June and make his own choice. I will just whisper the magic words Frühlingsgold, Nevada, Constance Spry and Maigold, the strongest rose I have ever grown, apricot in colour and smelling of coconuts, with two good flowerings every summer. I have a bush of Maigold on either side of a stone statue of Actaeon, the hunter who was turned by Artemis into a stag and devoured by his own hounds. The hunter of my statue is still in human shape, and every summer the Maigold branches join over his head and wreathe it in flowers. This is the only 'grand' effect in my whole garden, which is otherwise pure cottage, and I enjoy it unashamedly.

All the roses I have named I have grown or known personally, and can vouch for their behaviour; but there are many others suitable for the chalk garden – still more for the moderately limy garden – which the addict will discover for himself.

The choice of lilies in a chalk garden is more restricted, though lilies are ideal tub plants, and if you love some of the lime-hating varieties, this is the way to enjoy them.

Some years ago, I asked one of the lily growers at Chelsea which lilies he would recommend for my garden and he said crisply, 'None of them'. (That's the trouble with Chelsea – nobody has time to attend to you.) I now know he was wrong, but unfortunately he put me off experimenting for a long time, and my knowledge of lilies is recent and scanty, and mostly gathered from friends. His discouragement came at a bad moment when I had been tasting failure with Madonna lilies (*L. candidum*), and it was years before I took further advice. Even now, when I have read a good deal about lilies on lime, and consulted many gardeners, I am confused, because the answers are quite inconsistent. There are only a very few lilies to which *all* the chalk gardeners say 'yes'.

Outstanding among these is *L. henryi*, a spectacular lily from China with stems some five or six feet high bearing many orange-yellow flowers with long green anthers. They flower in August, and make the simplest garden look exotic.

L. regale is agreed by all to be chalk-tolerant; it is one of the loveliest of the white lilies, trumpet-shaped, flushed with purple outside and with yellow inside the throat.

L. testaceum passes the chalk test, an apricot lily with back-bent petals. And *L. martagon* (the Turk's-cap lily) and its varieties will flower well and spread freely if your garden has a dampish shady corner. It is the perfect lily for a wild garden.

On the wrong side of the coin, *L. auratum* and *L. sargentii* are agreed to be hopeless lilies on lime.

Between the two extremes are many lilies which may or may not be successful. P. de Jager, in their lily catalogue, list *L. hansonii* and *L. candidum* as being lime-tolerant. Four out of five chalk gardeners whom I consulted grow *L. hansonii* successfully, but only two feel that *L. candidum* is sound. I myself find that it comes up but never spreads – it's a case of one bulb, one flower, *ad infinitum* – and Lady Cranborne of Cranborne Manor has the same experience. Mrs Fish discarded it altogether and even the great Sir Frederick Stern found it grew poorly at Highdown. However, two cottage gardens in our district have great clumps of it; one must never be dogmatic.

De Jager also list *L. pardalinum*, the spotted orange lily, as lime-tolerant, but I would suspect this lily, too, as being hit-or-miss.

On the other hand, there are two flowers of the *Liliaceae* order which will give lily effects in the chalk garden with no difficulty, *Fritillaria imperialis*, the splendid Crown Imperial; and the mildly pleasing *Hemerocallis*, or Day Lily, which settles in any soil.

Other prominent mixed families are the magnolias, the primulas, the hydrangeas and the heathers.

The two best magnolias for chalk or lime are undoubtedly *M. soulangeana*, with large white waxy flowers flushed with purple, and *M. stellata*, with small starry flowers and a drugging scent. My own garden is too exposed for either, but both grow well in a chalk garden in Wiltshire which I often visit. As a general rule the chalk gardener should choose the Asiatic magnolias and avoid those of North American origin.

The primula family is divided, though the difference is often a matter of how much moisture each primula needs, rather than of lime tolerance. (Reginald Farrer divided primulas into 'dry-bobs' and 'wet-bobs'.) A chalk garden, with its quick drainage, is too dry for many primulas unless there is a pool or stream, when some of the marsh primulas can be grown.

In my own dry garden, auriculas (charming plants much loved by the Victorians) do well, and so do the common primroses and polyanthus, cowslips and the wild oxlip, *P. elatior*. This is almost the only plant in the garden which I can claim to be a Scott-James Special, for I don't know anyone else who grows it. It is somewhat like a cowslip, but much more decorative, with larger petals and a shorter calyx. I brought a few roots home one year from the Dordogne, where it grows abundantly in banks and beside the many streams of that lovely region, and now have a large colony. It likes rather heavy soil and I have planted it in an odd spot in the garden where there is a streak of clay.

The bog primulas, regrettably, are non-starters in my garden, and I can't consider such heavy drinkers as the handsome red candelabra primula, *P. japonica* or the tall sulphur-yellow Himalayan cowslip, *P. florindae*.

Other mixed families are the hydrangeas and the heathers. Most hydrangeas dislike lime, but *H. villosa* will grow to a fine size and the climbing hydrangea, *H. petiolaris*, will thrive, producing masses of white pannicles of flower and leaves of a particularly fresh green. The heathers are classic lime-haters, but the winter-flowering *E. carnea* will soon give your banks and braes a look of Bonnie

Scotland, if you want it. To me, a heather on downland is a fish out of water, but heathers are much in fashion, and doubtless I shall come round to the idea in time.

Plants I would like to grow (they are always Queen of the Party at the autumn shrub shows) are the Japanese maples, but they are simply not on. However, the Chinese *Acer griseum*, or Paperbark Maple, accepts lime and goes as fine an autumn colour as its Japanese relations. One should also think Chinese when choosing that beautiful dogwood, *Cornus kousa* – the variety *chinensis* is not only larger and finer than *C. kousa*, but does better on lime.

The smaller conifers, which one needs as a foil for deciduous shrubs, are not all easy customers, but it is worth knowing that in general the junipers are better for chalk than the cypresses. *Juniperus squamata* 'Meyeri' does extremely well on chalk, and the prostrate *J. pfitzeriana* has power mania and will smother a small garden if you let it.

Planting and Feeding

The choice of plants in a limy garden is not the only question. You can increase your range immensely if you cultivate your ground well. There are worse soils than chalk – I would hate to get bogged down in heavy clay – but it has certain demerits apart from its lime content. It dries out quickly, it is gluttonous for food and humus, and it tends to get short of nitrogen. You have to feed, feed, feed and mulch, mulch, mulch.

If you are starting a new garden on really poor ground with solid chalk near the surface, you will have to break up the soil to a depth of at least two feet and then consider how to feed it and improve its texture. You won't have any compost as yet, so you must try for farm manure or leafmould. If you can't get either, it would be best to import some loam, which will be fearfully expensive, but not as expensive or as sad as making great plantings which will die. You could also add peat, which does wonders for the texture of soil, but has no food value.

If you have reasonably good soil, you won't need these expensive imports, but you must still expect to feed and water your soil in perpetuity, for chalk is eternally hungry and thirsty.

Having prepared your soil, you must plant with particular care. Break up the soil to a good width and depth all round your planting hole, and work some manure or compost in with the soil, enough to last the plants for some time. Work peat in among the roots of all plants except the rare peat-haters. Give bulbs a handful of bonemeal. Give pinks some hoof-and-horn and lilies some sand under the bulb. The growers' catalogues will advise you on your plants' special tastes.

For after-care, you will need to feed the garden on the principles outlined in Chapter V, but even more lavishly. You must pack in bulky organic matter, for humus is quickly exhausted in limy soil. Two mulches a year are not too much.

When buying your organic-based fertilizer for spring use, choose one with a high nitrogen content, for most chalk gardens are short of nitrogen and the manure and compost you have to use are themselves de-nitrifying. And it is more important on chalk than on any other soil to give roses those three rose feeds a year.

The other special chalk problem is thirst. Moisture will not vanish so quickly as on a sandy soil, but it does drain fast in dry weather. There is a strong case for a peat mulch to conserve moisture, as suggested in Chapter V, but peat is horribly expensive. I usually go bust on enough peat to mulch the rose-beds, for you get no weeds all summer long and when the peat works down at last it makes the soil beautifully crumbly. I can think of nothing better than a sack of peat as a luxurious Christmas present for a gardening friend.

You will also have to be ready with the hose in dry weather, though in our part of England, as soon as we really need water, an edict usually goes out forbidding the use of the hose. The worried gardener then takes three baths a day instead of one and bails his bathwater into buckets which he carries into the garden, thus watering his plants and squaring his conscience.

Water all shrubs at the slightest sign of drought in their first year, before they have built up a good root system. Some shrubs, particularly lilacs, may need summer watering for the first two or three years. And water the lawn regularly. In my high, dry garden, I find that dried-up grass is the most intractable of problems – bare patches appear every summer, in spite of all the hosing and feeding. Next summer, I am going to try Mr Sydney Searle's system (see Chapter V) of leaving the clippings down, and if that doesn't work, I feel tempted to turn the whole place over to concrete.

PART IV

Other People's Views

CHAPTER XII

Eye Witness

As I wrote in the Foreword to this book, a notice saying 'GARDEN OPEN TODAY' is never likely to decorate my gate. But the diffidence I ought to feel in writing on gardening is tempered by the fact that I have seen many of England's most beautiful gardens and talked to many outstanding owner-gardeners. And when I talk to them, I don't just chat. I get out my notebook and grill them. I pinion them in the garden in mid-January asking about winter foliage when they would rather be indoors by the fire, and I prod them into the summer sun to identify their roses when a long, cool drink in the shade is more in their minds.

Interviewing a gardener is surprisingly difficult and requires much patience on both sides. This isn't because gardeners don't want to help, because they are a generous tribe. But the aesthetic side of gardening is largely intuitive, and very few gardeners analyse what they do. Only professional landscape designers or author-gardeners can explain a planting scheme. The amateur says 'I don't work the colours out, I just try this and that until I like it', or 'How often do I divide my irises? I dunno, whenever they seem to need it', or 'That's Euphorbia wodgermecallit, oh dear, my memory's getting frightful, we'll look it up later'.

Nonetheless, when two gardeners get together, the wish to

communicate is strong, and I have asked so many questions and seen so many gardens that I have collected some treasure in the way of ideas. Some of these may be familiar to the reader but others, I hope, will be new. I have tried some myself, with varying success, and there are others I want to try when I can raise the cash and that pearl beyond price, the skilled labour. I pass these ideas on in the hope that one or two will transplant into other gardens and prove, as the catalogues say, 'good doers'.

Design Ideas

Flowerbed Edgings. The scissor-sharp, public-park sort of edging to a bed may be suitable for shrub or rose beds, but with mixed borders, most of us like plants to spill over on to the path, breaking the hardness of the line. If the path is a grass one, this means ruination to the turf where the plants spill over it, and damage to the plants if the mower runs too close.

A ribbon of 'mowing stones' between the grass path and the border is a perfect solution, and need be no more than eight inches wide. At Cranborne Manor, hundreds of yards of grass paths have been edged with local stone – an expensive capital outlay, but on the other hand, the labour of trimming the edges is reduced for ever. In other gardens, I have seen mowing stones of synthetic stone which are quite pleasant to look at. In others, a double row of bricks is used, and is attractive if the bricks are old ones, but I would be afraid of weeds breaking through the cement and defeating the object.

Stepping Stones. I think Miss Jekyll did this first, though it may go back further, and it was a device used lavishly by Mrs Fish at East Lambrook Manor. Mrs Fish had a horror of treading on beds, especially on clay soil, as the trodden earth compacts and turns sour unless you prick every footmark with a fork as soon as you've made it. At East Lambrook, most of the flower beds are narrow enough to be worked from the paths, but the wider beds have stepping stones. Having seen them there, I copied the idea, and put little paths of stepping stones in the widest beds in my garden and find them extremely helpful, especially when the ground is sticky after rain. I used irregular-shaped pieces of York stone and think it worth the cost, as the colour is so mellow.

Varied Levels to Create Space. In Chapter II, I gave variety of levels as a cardinal principle of garden design. In a garden too small for levels to be changed achitecturally, it can be done with pots and troughs. In the tiny garden in South Kensington created by the late Mrs Cecily Mure (the front and back gardens each measure 25×35 feet), pots, troughs and raised beds carry the eye to many levels and give a third dimension and an illusion of space. They also allow far more plants to be grown than if the garden were flat. What might, in less sensitive hands, have been a garden of two dull patches, is in fact a connoisseur's garden crammed with rare shrubs, climbing and trailing plants, herbs, euphorbias, hellebores, hostas, camellias, succulents, rock plants and no fewer than forty clematis.

A Mount. This is the revival of an Elizabethan idea, when many gardens had a Mound or Mount, constructed by piling up soil into a hillock. Moving tons of soil, diverting streams or even (during the landscape frenzy of the 18th century) shifting inconvenient villages was no problem in the centuries of cheap labour. Today, a mount can *save* labour if you have a rubbish dump or pile of builder's rubble in your garden and can't face clearing it away.

At Crowdlesham House, Kemsing, in Kent, Mr John Cowell, Deputy Secretary of the Royal Horticultural Society, made a Mount in his father's garden to conceal an ancient rubbish dump, and the result is a highly decorative little hill planted with shrubs and ground cover, with a path to the summit from which the visitor can enjoy a view of the surrounding country. Mr Cowell and his brother constructed it as follows without any professional help.

First they piled the scattered ashes and débris of the dump into a higher and more compact shape and covered it with rough soil, the final size of the Mount being 12 feet high and 24 feet across the base. They then dug out the surface weeds, intending to plant it thickly enough to suppress further weeds, though ground elder and nettles recurred and had to be pulled out by hand. They made the initial error of not allowing for soil erosion, and later the soil began to subside after heavy rain. They rectified this by retaining the soil on the steepest side with seven rows of railway sleepers banked on top of each other.

After making the Mount, they planted, as though they were painting a picture. Light leaves against dark leaves, variegated leaves against glaucous leaves, spade-shaped leaves against the spindly needles of conifers. The shape of the bushes, as well as the colour, had to be interesting and they were planted for contrast; for instance, a *Viburnum tomentosum* 'Mariesii' makes a spreading shape which is punctuated by a spiky juniper. The Mount is topped with a Lawson cypress which is now 20 feet high and causing some anxiety because of its size. The shrubs below include dwarf cypresses and junipers, elaeagnus (plain and variegated), hebes, rhus, viburnums, cotoneasters, rosemary, berberis, escallonia, senecio, willow-leaf pear, buddleia and gorse. Foliage plants and ground cover include fennel, variegated grasses, hypericum, alchemilla, lamium, rodgersia and some fine groups of hostas.

Today, the planting is mature and so thick that the soil is completely covered, except for the path to the top, but the picture is not quite finished and never will be. As the plants grow, tall things are trimmed and invasive things eradicated, and the shapes and patterns are constantly improved. The Mount is a fine piece of planting which is beautiful from every side and which provides a pleasant look-out from the top – all made from a rubbish dump by two busy young men in their spare time.

Corners. Few gardeners today can cope with mass plantings of flowers and many don't even want to, getting more pleasure from small plantings and separate 'corners'. Mr John Piper's cottage garden has not only 'separate rooms' in front of the house, as described in Chapter II, but an amazing number of corners and alcoves elsewhere. The farmhouse is rich in outbuildings, some old and some built-on – sheds, studios and stables stick out all over the place – and wherever two walls meet, there is a corner flower-bed or a small wild planting.

One such corner is all white and green, which is to Mr Piper the most important colour in the garden. In this, an old damson tree, with a Paul's Lemon Pillar rose and honeysuckle growing up it, is underplanted with euphorbias and hellebores. Another corner has a pear-tree underplanted with lilies-of-the-valley, *Helleborus foetidus*, rosemary and thyme. A magnolia is underplanted with Mr Piper's 'thistle nursery', for he has a passion for the thistle family. One corner has a bush of *Spiraea arguta* growing quite happily with kitchen rhubarb.

His garden would shock the 'keep-your-garden-open-to-get-a-sense-of-space' school, but it is endlessly interesting and there is some corner flowering whenever you go there.

Not everyone can provide corners, for the basic buildings may not be there, but corners are worth more consideration than they get. I am sure that the corners provided by the smallest shed should not be wasted.

Paths. Some gardeners like their paths to go undeviatingly from A to B, but something more ambiguous adds greatly to the interest of a garden. Mr Geoffrey Gorer, who has a large, finely planted garden in Sussex, has designed it so that you always come to a *choice of paths*. Main paths divide into subsidiary paths so that you may, for instance, on your way from the house to the rhododendron garden, change your mind and turn aside to the rose garden or the pond. Mr Gorer chose his house because the soil was acid. He had previously gardened on alkaline soil and longed to specialize in rhododendrons and camellias. He now has over 500 varieties of rhododendron, including some of his own breeding, flowering from January to August.

A Herb Garden in Town. There are three conventional kinds of town garden: a central lawn surrounded by shrub or flower beds; a 'rus in urbe' cottage planting, once rare in towns but now increasingly popular; and the 'room outdoors' style, with most of the garden paved and 'plants used as infill'.

One of the most charming town gardens I have seen is none of these: it is something quite fresh. Mr Hardy Amies' garden in Kensington is inspired by Tudor herb gardens. It is formal, the design being of squares within squares. The garden measures 60 feet by 30 feet, has a minute grass plot in the centre surrounded by narrow beds planted with espalier pears. Round this is a flagged path and outside the path are beds divided into very small sections and filled with herbs – some 80 varieties in all. The plants include many mints, thymes, rosemaries, hyssop, lovage, foxgloves and sweet woodruff – every plant has to be culinary, medicinal or aromatic to be allowed a place.

The outer fences are covered with climbers, especially roses, so that the geometric formality is softened.

The end of the garden furthest from the house contains a wide bed for tender herbs, including twenty-eight varieties of scented geranium, and a plastic frame is pulled over them in winter, and gentle heat switched on, turning the bed into a small conservatory.

A Country Herb Garden. The garden of Alderley Grange, in Gloucestershire, is one of the finest pieces of post-war plantsmanship. Consisting of two large walled gardens, derelict save for some fine old trees, it was taken over in 1962 by Mr and Mrs James Lees-Milne and planted with a profusion of old-fashioned roses, border perennials and foliage plants. It looked, some eight years later, as if it had been established for fifty years.

One of the most attractive features is the herb garden, which is symmetrical, divided by brick paths into 8 wedge-shaped segments, all edged with dwarf box. Inside each segment is a luxuriant bush of the damask rose Ispahan, surrounded by herbs. A formal design is traditional for a herb garden, for herbs are the oldest English garden plants, grown during the centuries when all gardens were neat, geometric plots.

Planting Ideas

Hedges and Edges. Hedges are not only boundaries, they can be part of the garden architecture. They can be grown as internal walls, as buttresses, as gateways, as frames to alcoves and statues, or as decorative edgings. Of all the hedging plants, few are better than box, which is both reliable and tractable, like an ideal husband.

Some of the most interesting box plantings in England are at Haseley Court, a very large garden in Oxfordshire. The celebrated set of topiary chessmen at Haseley, cut in box and yew, is very old, but Mrs Nancy Lancaster, who bought and transformed the house and garden in the 'fifties, made many new box plantings which are both decorative and labour-saving. Mrs Lancaster comes from Virginia, where clipped box is a garden tradition.

In one part of the garden she used box as walls to cut up a long, wide herbaceous border. She found the border too large to plant and manage and divided it into alcoves by planting 4-foot box hedges at intervals *across* the border. It is much easier to plant separate alcoves than a long unbroken sweep.

In the main walled garden at Haseley, box is used extensively as edging. The centrepiece of this garden is a mosaic of small geometric beds in the Italian style, every bed box-edged. Though the design is formal, the planting is not. The stiff beds have been quite loosely planted with such things as old roses, tobacco plant, alchemilla, sweet rocket and self-seeded columbines. The informal planting of formal beds seems to me very contemporary.

The whole 12-acre garden is run with only two gardeners, and though weeding, pruning and tidying at Haseley may get behind-hand, it always looks elegant. Box acts as a third gardener.

(I myself have found in my cottage garden that box is supreme for pulling a sprawling garden together. I have improved the front garden considerably by scrapping the beds either side of the front path (though planted to match they always, through some quirk of the slope or the light, managed to flower at different times) and planting low hedges of clipped box in their place. Planted 18 inches apart, the bushes took three years to join up, but after two years they had made an embryo hedge.)

In another garden where hedges are used as architecture, they are grown almost like castle walls. At Charleston Manor, some of the tall, thick yew hedges have projecting buttresses, all of yew, and windows cut in the hedges for looking out on the scene below.

At Garsington Manor, near Oxford, thick yew hedges have niches in them for statues.

The pleaching of trees and hedges is an interesting revival, though not easy to do – it calls for professional skill. For sheer panache, I have never seen anything to surpass the avenue at Haseley of pleached hornbeams which merge into pleached laburnums. When the laburnums are in flower in May or June, you look down a long green tunnel which seems to be ablaze with golden sunlight at the end. This pleached walk was planted only ten years ago, a reminder that great gardens do not take an eternity to make.

For those who are not colour-mad, restful enclosures can be made by hedges surrounding nothing but grass, an idea which descends from the bowling alley. At The Deanery, Sonning-on-Thames, where the house and garden were designed by Sir Edwin Lutyens and the garden planted by Miss Jekyll, there is a long lawn surrounded by yew hedges with a stone seat at the far end; it was originally a bowling alley. No bowling now, but the enclosure is still attractive and should appeal to any gardener who can get his lawn and hedges trimmed, but is too busy to grow flowers.

At Cranborne Manor, too, where there are many hedged enclosures, some contain nothing but lawn.

At Hidcote, there is a circular garden of grass only, enclosed by a 12-foot mixed hedge of box and yew. And at Glenveagh, a spectacular scenic garden in County Donegal, full of rare and semi-tropical trees and shrubs, one simple enclosure always evokes special delight – just an evergreen hedge enclosing grass and a Scots pine tree, the grass left long enough for the daisies to flower.

For an internal hedge (not a thick boundary hedge) roses or flowering shrubs make a decorative change from the usual stout hedging plants. At Sulhamstead Rectory, there is a glorious and unusual hedge of the crimson tree paeony, *Paeonia delavayi*.

Colour Schemes. Some gardeners dislike planned colour schemes. John Piper is one of them. Others, of the Jekyll school, think of every planting as a picture. Most of the gardens where I have thought the colours most harmonious include plenty of white flowers.

At Glyndebourne, one of the best borders is of white flowers against the background of a high yew hedge. (There is, of course, a narrow grass path between.) Huge white delphiniums, white campanulas, paeonies, Oriental poppies, *Crambe cordifolia*, tradescantia, hardy geraniums, galega and marguerites keep the border filled for most of the summer.

At The Old Rectory, Burghfield, Berkshire, Mrs Ralph Merton has planted a fine double herbaceous border, 60 feet long, with traditional brilliant colours, but she cools them off with white. She finds that flowers never clash if white is used between them, and the border holds white irises, marguerites, paeonies, lilies and phlox to act as go-betweens. The only colour not used in these borders is orange.

I tried this white recipe in my own border, but something went wrong with the timing. I have a scarlet *Rosa moyesii* which flowers next to and simultaneously with a clump of magenta *Geranium psilostemon*, and though I pretended that this was a colour scheme Bakst would have liked, in fact they clashed furiously. So I put a clump of snow-white bearded irises between them, with exquisite results – for one day. Then the wretched irises faded, as the rose and the geranium came to their peak.

At Cranborne Manor there is a white garden, as at Sissinghurst, but in this case, the white is warmed with apricot. There are flowers in every shade of white, from ice white to Devonshire cream: white shrub roses and climbers, white martagon lilies, valerian, Oriental poppies, petunias, salvias, pansies, astrantias, cottage pinks, crambe, white ground-cover and green-and-white hosta foliage, relieved by the apricot splashes of honeysuckle and roses like Buff Beauty.

Another colour idea which always succeeds is the use of purple foliage plants. In the Red and Purple Garden at Hidcote, there are deep curved borders of red plants with splashes of purple – purple nut-trees, purple sage and *Acer plantanoides* 'Crimson King'. The effect is brilliant, but not fiery, because there is green foliage to cool it down. At Burghfield Rectory, there is one soft grey border enlivened with purple violas, purple-leaved sage and the purple-leaved clover which enjoys the name of *Trifolium repens* 'Purpurascens Quadriphyllum'. At Kiftsgate, purple sage is freely used in the herbaceous borders and as corner clumps in the rose-beds.

Another quite different colour scheme which I have enjoyed is at St Columb's, the Donegal home of Mr Derek Hill. The house, perched on a hill overlooking a lake, is painted Venetian red, and it is surrounded with a footmuff of dark evergreens. Mahonias, cotoneasters, *Viburnum davidii* and a thick edging of bergenias clothe the lower edges of the walls.

That fine gardener and naturalist, Mr H. E. Bates, is particularly good with garden colours, using dark conifers as a background to spring-flowering shrubs. At his cottage at Little Chart, Kent, there is an island bed about 24 feet long, with two cypresses, *Chamaecyparis lawsoniana* 'Fletcheri', as background to the creamy yellow flowers of *Cytisus praecox*, and to primulas, Bleeding Heart, irises, columbines, potentillas and sedums in due course.

A delectable rose planting suggested by Mr James Russell, of The Dairies, Castle Howard, is mixed yellow and white shrub roses. He likes a mass planting of yellow Frühlingsgold and white Nevada to flower in unison at the end of May.

Underplanting of Roses. It is becoming increasingly recognized that rose-bushes are not a total, all-year-round dream of beauty. Many roses when not in flower are all bare, thorny legs, and a rose-bed is much improved with an edging of interesting plants, or with scattered clumps of underplanting.

At Great Haseley, a wide rose border is unconventionally edged with a thick band of golden variegated grass: other rose-beds here are underplanted with clumps of white and ink-blue pansies.

At Cranborne Manor, roses are underplanted with clumps of lavender or cottage pinks. At Basildon Park, Berkshire, a formal octagonal garden is surrounded by a hedge of rugosa roses with a thick edging of alpine strawberries at their feet. At The Old Rectory, Sulhamstead, a bed of Iceberg roses is edged with calamint, and a bed of Allgold roses is underplanted with occasional clumps of variegated box. At Jay's Cottage, Tisbury, Wiltshire, an old cottage with a downland garden, Dr Frank Tait underplants roses with clumps of green-and-white apple mint, frequently clipped to keep their cushion shape.

A bonus advantage of a thick, evergreen edging to rose-beds is that it makes it difficult for the birds to scatter manure and mulches on to the surrounding paths. I have found myself that 'Lamb's Ear' works very well.

Other Rose Ideas. I had always supposed, until I saw it many years after first hearing tell of it, that the famous *Rosa filipes* 'Kiftsgate' at Kiftsgate Manor was planted to climb up some lofty tree. Not at all. The rose is grown as a shrub, that is to say, it is free-standing, and is as tall and strong as a full-grown may-tree. Another sensation at Kiftsgate is a double hedge of the red-and-white striped rose, *Rosa mundi*, bordering a grass path. This garden has one of the finest collections of old roses to be seen anywhere.

A happy rose mixture is shrub roses with wild plants, especially foxgloves, an idea I read in *The Old Shrub Roses*, by Graham Thomas and took up very successfully, sowing foxglove seeds round a group of *Rosa rubrifolia*.

Climbers Grown as Sprawlers. Most climbing plants are willing to grow downwards as well as upwards, and often a sprawling plant is exactly what is wanted on a sloping site.

On the Mount, at Kemsing, which I have already described, a *Hydrangea petiolaris* is planted half-way up the slope without support and is allowed to tumble down, covering the ground with its fresh green leaves and with large white flowers in June. At Kiftsgate, a honeysuckle is used as a sprawler, covering a stone path with June blossom. At St Columb's, climbers like New Dawn and Albertine and honeysuckle are grown over tree stumps and then left to sprawl. One stump is a mass of *Rosa filipes* and ferns. The vine, *Vitis coignetiae*, can also be grown downhill.

In terraced gardens, rambler roses can be grown at the top of a wall and allowed to shower over it. I have seen Albertine, Albéric Barbier and Dr van Fleet used in this way, and Miss Jekyll often used the semi-white double rose, The Garland, at the top of a wall, allowing it to grow up some five feet and then to fall downhill.

Border Troubles. Most gardeners would agree that the herbaceous border is the part of the garden most likely to fail. Borders require a lot of work and a dozen things can go wrong. Either the planting is spotty, or bad weather spoils your plans, or the whole thing is over too soon, leaving dead stalks and dying leaves instead of the Grocer's Calendar picture you had hoped for. The advice given to me on borders was meagre, for many good gardeners have opted out, but the few hints I received are good.

When I was grumbling about my own border, Mr H. E. Bates suggested that I was trying to bring it on too soon. No one border can be full of colour for more than three months (Miss Jekyll's gardens had several borders), and Mr Bates's own border does not get into swing before July, is at its peak in mid-August, and goes on through September. He suggests, as favourite border plants, many of the salvias, *Verbena bonariensis, Polygonum amplexicaule,* the Steel Globe Thistle, *Echinops ritro,* eryngium or Sea Holly, *Hebe* 'Midsummer Beauty', the heleniums, *Artemisia lactiflora* and *A.* 'Lambrook Silver', solidago, phloxes and penstemons. I am trying to follow his advice and move my early plants out of the border, but my garden is so crowded I don't know where they can go.

Several gardeners suggest that a border is more romantic if the vista is broken, not all seen at once, and the division of a long border into sections certainly makes it easier to manage.

I have already described (under Hedges and Edges) how one border at Haseley is divided into bays. At the Old Rectory, Sulhamstead, the vista is broken by arching shrubs which spray over on to the paths like fountains. *Rosa moyesii* and Blanc Double de Coubert are used at one point, and a group of *Cornus alba sibirica* 'Spaethii' at another.

The staking of plants is a hated border job, and is reduced as much as possible. Some gardeners use a maximum of plants which don't need staking, like phlox, Knee-hi sweet peas and the shorter achilleas. Others make the work as light as possible by using peasticks for lightweight plants and the labour-saving wire stakes with circles at the top for heavier plants. These are not unsightly for long as the leaves soon cover them.

A way to avoid the fatal bitty look in a border is to have middling high groups in front of the border, not to graduate down to excessively dwarf plants. No small plants are used in the famous borders at Kiftsgate. A way to avoid untidiness is to cut down foliage after flowering more ruthlessly than the textbooks allow. Oriental poppies can be cut down straight away, and I find that *Euphorbia epithymoides*, which gets very heavy and bushy after flowering, comes to no harm at all if the outer stalks are cut away.

All gardeners stress the importance of deadheading the border almost every day.

Probably one of Miss Jekyll's principles is the most helpful advice of all – to make your groups of plants lozenge-shaped, not round, and to have them running parallel with the border, not across it. A glance at her planting plans confirms that this was her usual method.

The Unweeded Garden. A garden which will, I think, become one of the most famous gardens of the 'seventies, is that of Mr Keith Steadman, at Wickwar, Gloucestershire. This contoured Cotswold garden is never weeded, pruned or sprayed. It is planted with groups and single specimens of very choice shrubs, small trees and old roses, perfectly placed in rough-cut grass. There are no edges to the beds, the shrubs go their own way, the plants are all-important, the work is minimal. There is also a small formal garden so thickly planted that the after-care is next-to-nothing – simply seasonal mulching and the removal of surplus plants when the beds get too crowded.

Grass Contrasts. A simple planting idea is often the best, and one of the most effective I have seen is the contrast of close-mown grass with rough-cut grass. The line where the close-cutting stops can be an important element in the garden design, giving straight lines, or curves, or whatever's wanted. Two lengths of grass are well used at Scotney Castle, home of the late and well-loved Mr Christopher Hussey. The terrace behind the house has wide steps and gently sloping banks leading down to a lawn. The lawn is mown close but the banks are rough-cut, a contrast which delighted Mr Hussey's perceptive eye.

Moving to Indoor Quarters. Lady Cranborne of Cranborne Manor says that scented-leaved geraniums are the best of all house plants, much easier than cyclamen or azaleas, which wilt in warm rooms. In summer, there are many clumps of sweet geraniums in the borders, adding to the scents in this fragrant garden, but they are not hardy and in the autumn they are dug up and planted in pots and bowls for the house.

An Edible Alpine. Of the many alpine plants used as 'paving plants', the most hospitable is the alpine strawberry. At Holt Rectory, Norfolk, strawberries are stuffed into paving cracks and edge the terraces, for guests to help themselves. Birds do not seem to steal this fruit. The variety to order is 'Baron Solemacher', which increases by clumping and forms no runners.

Tubs and Pots. Most of us think of these as terrace accessories, but at Alderley Grange, Mrs Lees-Milne has flower-filled tubs and pots at innumerable points in the garden. This is a very profuse and richly planted garden, and the pots are a sort of bonus pleasure, as though the beds simply couldn't contain their plants and they needed an annexe.

Plant Associations. One visits gardens for two reasons, to enjoy what one sees and to get ideas for one's own garden. Of these, it is the plant associations that are most easily memorized.

The most famous plant associations have been seen by so many people and photographed so often that it would be pointless for me to recall them again. I have tried to select a few planting ideas which are not too well-known.

At Hidcote, I saw an interesting group of mahonias in early March, when the garden is not normally open. One tall *M.* 'Charity' was encircled with a few bushy plants of *M. aquifolium*, which provided a perfect cover-up for its long, bare main stem.

At The Old Vicarage, Bucklebury, a beautifully planted informal garden with a Henry Moore reclining figure looking away from the garden out on to the open fields, a fine old yew-tree is underplanted with *Cyclamen neapolitanum*. They seem to like the thin, bare soil and make pink and white ribbons in the yew's deep shadow.

At The Old Rectory, Sulhamstead, Irish yews are brilliantly used in combination with cypresses. A long vista ends in a semi-circle of Irish yews and cypresses, which enclose a stone urn nestling among lilies and hostas (*L. pardalinum* and *H. sieboldiana*). (See Plate II.)

At St Columb's, where shrubs are planted to make contrasts of shape, colour and density, one particularly good small group is of an Irish yew, contrasted (for shape) with a prostrate juniper and (for colour) with a variegated dogwood.

Planting for Shelter. Shrub experts tell me that quite tender shrubs can be grown in quite windy places if you plant tougher shrubs to protect them. At Westonbirt School, large yews put a sheltering arm round camellias. (The camellia plant is perfectly hardy but the flowers are not and can be ruined by frost.) At Kew Gardens, rhododendrons make a windbreak for such tender subjects as *Daphne odora*.

At Buckingham Palace, large new plantings of ornamental shrubs were begun in about 1960, to replace the dreary laurels, privets and hollies which had been there for decades. But the offending shrubs were not dug out straight away, but were left to shelter the young camellias, azaleas, mahonias, hybrid rhododendrons, choisya and pieris that were being planted instead. As the young shrubs grew up, the old background shrubs were removed, but as a gradual process.

Strictly Technical

Bulb Planting. There is no source of practical advice better than a crack head gardener, if you can find one with patience to listen to you. I was once lucky enough to spend a morning with Mr F. C. Nutbeam, head gardener at Buckingham Palace, who showed me, among other things, how to 'tongue' turf when planting bulbs in grass. As one thousand crocuses is a small planting in the Palace garden, it is important to do the job with the best possible technique.

You choose your spot for a group of three, five or seven bulbs (always an uneven number), and you turn back the turf leaving a tongue still attached to the soil. Then you plant, replace the turf and make slits for the bulbs to come through, so that they don't lift the turf as they grow.

On the subject of bulb naturalization, Mrs Fish told me that tulips could be left instead of lifted if you planted them very deeply in the first place. Though Darwin tulips would never naturalize as well as smaller tulips, even these could be left undisturbed if planted deep enough.

Composting. The various methods are well documented, but Mr Nutbeam gave me one nugget of news, that the leaves of some trees, notably plane and sycamore, are uncompostable – they don't rot and they sour the soil. In the league table, he put beech and oak at the top for compost, with elm quite usable if you wait rather longer. I find our elm leaves rot in a year.

Stratification. I am indebted to Mr H. E. Bates for all my stock of *Helleborus corsicus* and for some young plants of *Paeonia mlokosewitschii* which are coming along nicely, all grown from seed which he kindly sent me with instructions for growing them outdoors, without a greenhouse or frame, by 'stratification'. This bring-'em-up-tough method is suitable for seeds with a hard outer covering.

You sow the seeds after collection in a box or pan filled with sandy soil, water them well, cover the box with a pane of glass and put it outside the house against a north wall. Then you leave them alone and do nothing further until about Christmas, when you take off the glass and subject the pan to frost and snow. This softens the hard seed covering and you hope for germination in the spring. I admit I expected nothing, and was amazed when a fine crop of *H. corsicus* seedlings came up in March and grew into plants which flower abundantly every year. In the case of the paeonies, the seedlings came up in March *a year later*, and it was only because I was too lazy to clear away the box that they survived. When at last I was in a tidying mood and picked up the box to throw the contents away, there were a dozen healthy seedlings of 'Mlok'. It will be another few years before I enjoy their lovely pale yellow flowers, but I am nursing them on their way.

Equipment. An idea of my own – that for the busy, feeble or just lazy owner-gardener, much more use could be made of very sharp knives as garden tools. I am devoted to a large kitchen knife and to a boy-scout or cowboy knife left over from a period when my children were never seen without a selection of knives stuck into leather belts.

The kitchen knife is ideal for dividing lilies-of-the-valley, cutting back ground-cover plants and for any other jobs where the orthodox instructions are 'Take a sharp spade'. I have never yet found a spade sharp enough to cleave through lily-of-the-valley roots or to make a clean cut in the advancing armies of lamium, sweet woodruff or alchemilla.

The scout knife is perfect (this will make purists shudder) for planting bulbs in grass. I used to find that planting a few dozen daffodils in our tight turf could take a morning. With a quick twist of the knife. I can make a hole in a matter of seconds, waggling it about at the bottom of the hole to ensure that there is no air pocket.

Pruning. I have another theory of my own, about pruning neglected shrubs, such as lilacs or forsythia which have got leggy. One is usually told to cut them back hard 'sacrificing a year's flower', but this is a thing I can't bear to do. If one spreads the job over three years, cutting back a third at a time, one improves the bush in the end without the awful sacrifice of flowers. Besides, one is getting older. I may not *be* there the year after next.

Fencing for Windbreak. One of the prettiest small gardens in England belongs to that fine writer and plantswoman, Miss Christine Kelway, whose cottage at Trebetherick, Cornwall, is right on the sea. Yet, on that fierce North Cornish coast, the garden is cosy and protected. Miss Kelway told me that the most efficient possible windbreak is a slatted fence, with the slats 1 inch wide and 1 inch apart, which protects within a distance of eight times its height. A fence with apertures to let some of the wind through is better than a solid fence or wall which forces the wind to go over the top.

Planting. It is a sound idea always to carry round with you when planting a bucket of a suitable mixture to work into the soil. Mrs Fish, who worked on heavy marl, never moved without a bucket of mixed peat and sand. Others take a bucket of bonemeal mixed with compost or manure.

Circles of Soil. All the gardeners I have talked to, professionals and amateurs, have stressed the importance of leaving a generous circle of cultivated soil round shrubs, roses or fruit trees planted in grass for at least two years after planting. One nursery will not consider replacing dead plants unless a circle at least 4 feet in diameter has been left for trees and at least 3 feet for small shrubs. In gardens celebrated for their shrub roses, I always observed round every rose a good circle of cultivated soil accessible to air, rain and supplies of food.

Knowing Your Garden. They call it 'knowing your micro-climate' and it is the most important advice of all. Have your soil tested for acidity in two or three places. Study the winds and draughts, the hours of sunshine and the shadows, and find the warm and cool spots. Don't struggle with plants which hate your garden, but on the other hand, don't be put off by the gloomy predictions of other gardeners. A maxim of Mr Geoffrey Gorer's is 'Never believe anything is tender until you've killed it yourself'.

CHAPTER XIII

A Gardener's Bookshelf

It is customary to end a book with a bibliography – a catalogue of every conceivable book connected with the subject – but I don't think any reader would thank me for listing all the gardening books I have read. The total body of horticultural literature is enormous, and although my own reading is only a drop in the ocean, I have spent more hours in libraries than most gardeners would want to spend away from their plants.

A lot of this literature is expendable. It's not rubbish – the stuffing is usually there – but many books are repetitive or overlapping, or grindingly pedestrian in style, or badly produced, and some are flashly illustrated and not worth their hefty price.

Yet, since reading is one of the two best ways of learning about gardening (the other is visiting gardens), I thought I would end my own book with a piece of literary weeding and suggest a bookshelf for the gardener who, like myself, thirsts for accurate information but can't take anything too technical, nor enjoy those plodding books which seem to have been written by the author's gum-booted feet.

I have not relied solely on my own judgment. I have had the good fortune to browse in the libraries of many outstanding gardeners, and have found that in house after house the chosen books are much the same. Out of the thousands of gardening books published, a select few have floated to the top. Of course, in an advanced botanist's library, there will be specialist books and monographs and floras in addition to the general favourites, but in the houses of the gifted amateurs, the book corner is usually quite small. Of all the books read, a chosen few have been preserved, and these few are in constant use.

What would constitute a good bookshelf? Every gardener will want some basic reference books; some books which are lovable – the beautifully written books which you thumb and re-thumb and hate to lend out of the house; one or two illustrated books of genuine aesthetic quality; and a selection of the best of the growers' catalogues. Ideas are given at the end of this chapter on how to lay your hands on books which are out of print.

Basic Reference Books

The standard reference book on plants is *The Royal Horticultural Society Dictionary of Gardening*, which consists of four volumes and a supplement and is an essential possession for anyone who is interested in the nomenclature and identification of plants. The practical gardener may think it too costly an investment and he will be very well served indeed by *Sanders' Encyclopaedia of Gardening*, revised by A. G. L. Hellyer, which gives you in a single volume a brief description and cultural notes on most of the plants you are likely to grow.

The other great reference work for those who can afford it is W. J. Bean's *Trees and Shrubs Hardy in the British Isles*, one of the great gardening classics which is now being republished volume by volume, edited and brought up to date by Sir George Taylor of Kew Gardens. It is a lovely thing to own, especially in this age of shrub gardening, for it is both well written and well illustrated. All the science is there, but so are the late W. J. Bean's highly personal comments and opinions.

Supplement your major textbooks with some of the Collins Guides on the subjects which interest you most, for they are both comprehensible and sound. Titles include *Border Plants*, by Frances Perry, *Bulbs*, by Patrick M. Synge, and *Roses*, by Bertram Park. Three other notable books on particular plants are *Irises*, by Harry Randall, *Hardy Ferns*, by Reginald Kaye and *Climbing Plants for Walls and Gardens*, by C. E. Lucas Phillips.

All these are books about plants, and the owner-gardener also needs some how-to-do-it books; of these, the Penguin Books produced for the R.H.S. are the best possible value for money. There's one on *Herbaceous Plants*, by Lanning Roper, one on *The Cool Greenhouse*, by G. W. Robinson, *Rock Gardens*, by E. B. Anderson, *Water Gardens*, by Frances Perry, *Gardening the Modern Way*, by Roy Hay, *Tree Fruit Growing*, by Raymond Bush, and many more, all by writers whose names are household words. The small R.H.S. booklets are also useful and incredibly cheap. *Pruning Hardy Shrubs*, by A. Osborn, is essential literature for the price of a bus fare, listing the common garden shrubs and telling you in a few words when and how to prune each kind. Most experts make pruning sound so complicated that you shudder to take up the knife, but Mr Osborn makes it sound perfectly simple, which it is. *Ground Cover Plants*, by Graham Thomas, is another excellent booklet in the series, a triumph of compressed information about permanent gardening, with handsome photographs in colour and black and white.

For practical information, the Studio Vista books on specialized subjects are also excellent, notably *Growing Vegetables*, by David Pople, *Hardy Perennials*, by Christopher Lloyd and *Climbing Plants*, by Richard Gorer.

I personally prefer a number of specialized books to an all-round compendium, partly because I like small books to read in bed; but if you like a lot in one volume, I suggest the *Reader's Digest Encyclopaedia of Garden Plants and Flowers*, which the publishers rightly say is the Mrs Beeton of gardening. Descriptions, growing instructions and possible problems are given for a very wide range of plants, with plenty of illustrations.

There are also some good reference books available for those with a special sort of garden. *The Small Garden*, by C. E. Lucas Phillips, is the acknowledged classic on the subject. *Seaside Gardening*, by Christine Kelway, who lives on the Cornish coast, is expert and elegantly written. *A Chalk Garden*, by F. C. Stern, who created Highdown, is invaluable to chalk gardeners, the story of a garden of beauty and botanic interest made out of virgin chalk. And there are a number of knowledgeable books on herb gardens most of which are spoilt for me by their archness of style – in order to get at the facts about tarragon and the various mints, you have to go through a lot of whimsy about ye olde remedies and witches' brewes. One of the most useful and straightforward is *A Book of Herbs*, by Dawn Macleod.

Apart from plant reference books and how-to-do-it books, the serious gardener needs to know something about garden history and styles. *A History of British Gardening*, by Miles Hadfield, is both scholarly and digestible, and it increases one's pleasure in visiting old gardens to know how they came into being. For potted information, *The Shell Gardens Book*, edited by Peter Hunt, is first-class, a treasury of compressed information about the history of English gardening, garden styles, architecture, designers and plantsmen, with notes on the most important gardens in Great Britain and Ireland. And if you love visiting gardens, you will need the three guide-books of gardens open to the public: *Historic Houses, Castles and Gardens in Great Britain and Ireland, Gardens of England and Wales Open to the Public*, sponsored by the National Gardens Scheme, and *Gardens to Visit*, sponsored by the Gardeners' Sunday Organization. There is also *Gardens of Scotland*, on the same lines. The first of these is devoted to large, grand gardens, including National Trust gardens, while many of the gardens which are open for charity, listed in the other booklets, are smaller and less formal. All these guides are brought up to date every year, and if you don't have them in your bookshelf, then keep them in your car.

Lovable Books

These are the books which do more than instruct, they communicate a love of gardening. Regrettably, most of the lovable books were written a long time ago and many are out of print.

The greatest of them all, to my mind, is E. A. Bowles' trilogy, *My Garden in Spring, My Garden in Summer* and *My Garden in Autumn and Winter*, from which many of the best gardeners I know learned their first lessons. The first of the three volumes has a delightful introduction by Reginald Farrer. Early editions of these books are now rather rare and I was lucky enough to get a set in 1969 for £18, but once you have read them you will go to any lengths to own them, and will then dig into them on many a winter's night and imagine yourself out in the sunshine with your plants. For nobody has ever written so well about plants as Mr Bowles, who was both a fine botanist and a stylist who could stand up in the best literary company. He describes gardening, and plants, and the little social incidents in a gardener's life with affection and humour but never descends to being whimsical or lush.

Mr Bowles kept one corner of his garden for crazy plants and called it the Lunatic Asylum. 'Yet another elder has been certified insane and admitted to this select company. Its madness consists in the greater portion of the lamina of the leaf blades being reduced to a mere thread, and it looks as though an army of locusts or caterpillars had halted to dine on it, but for all that has rather a soft, ferny look from a distance.' 'The *Allium dioscoridis* possesses the most pungent and evil smell of any plant I know, and I enjoy breaking a leaf in half and getting my friends to help in deciding whether it most resembles an escape of gas or a new mackintosh.' 'I must provide *Helleborus niger* with shade, and moisture beyond that of the atmosphere, if I wish it to "grow for me", as Irish gardeners say so pleasantly. I like the personal reciprocal touch in these words. How different a vision of mutual understanding they conjure up from that mild reproach and suggestion of wilful suicide in the other Hibernian phrase, "It died on me", which so neatly lays the blame on the plant.' Very good writing, this, and I shall spoil it for you if I go on quoting.

In *My Garden in Spring*, there is a long botanical passage on the dissection of a snowdrop bulb which is one of the most lucid pieces of scientific writing I have ever read, and in *My Garden in Autumn and Winter* an equally clear explanation of why leaves colour in autumn and how evergreen trees protect their leaves in winter.

All serious gardeners have read *The English Flower Garden*, by William Robinson, which I consider essential background reading, and most would think it worth owning. In this amusing, irritable classic, first published in 1883, an Irishman who became one of the great revolutionaries of garden history expounds his theory of natural gardening in strong, astringent language, and attacks the artificial formal gardening which was fashionable with the Victorians. His friend, Miss Jekyll, is not so good a writer, but *Wood and Garden* and *Colour in the Flower Garden* should be read all the same, for Miss Jekyll was steeped in plantsmanship, the greatest herbaceous planter there has ever been. It is fascinating to discover how many modern practices started with her, such as the propping up of herbaceous plants with peasticks instead of stakes, and how many of today's foliage plants, like hostas and bergenias, were favourite Jekyll plant material.

Some gardeners, especially collectors, grow very fond of the writings of the plant-explorers who headed the great expeditions between about 1890 and 1930, and spent years in the remote and dangerous corners of the world hunting and classifying new species.

The literary style of these explorers is sometimes on the heavy side, but the romance of their adventures survives the mannered prose. Reginald Farrer spent two years, starting in 1913, exploring the wild borders of North West China and Tibet, travelling by sedan chair, mule train and on foot in mountain country infested by brigands, and one shares his ecstasy every time his hardships are rewarded by the sight of new flowers, many of which were later to be honoured by the epithet *farreri*. His story of the expedition, called *On the Eaves of the World*, throws some curious sidelights on the organization of the Chinese Empire in 1913. Another book by Farrer, *The English Rock Garden*, published in 1919, is still the alpine gardener's bible.

Farrer is usually considered the best writer among the collectors, but Frank Kingdon Ward was a better botanist and discovered many more new plants; if you have a taste for this aspect of gardening, try his *The Land of the Blue Poppy* or *Plant Hunting on the Edge of the World*.

Luckily, not all lovable books were written long ago and not all are hard to come by. Still in print are *The Old Shrub Roses* and *Plants for Ground Cover*, both by Graham Stuart Thomas, one of the finest gardeners of our time and Gardens Adviser to the National Trust; V. Sackville West's *Garden Book*, a unique combination of earthy knowledge and elegant writing; *The Well-Tempered Garden* and *Foliage Plants*, by Christopher Lloyd; and most of the books of Margery Fish, which I pick up again and again because she loves her plants so dearly and writes about the crowded, cottagey sort of garden I like best. *Carefree Gardening* and *A Flower for Every Day* are books which inspire you to be a better gardener yourself. If you read one in bed at night, you will be rushing out next morning with trug and trowel looking for bare spaces to fill with Mrs Fishy plants. Mrs Fishery is a cult, and I'm a member.

Illustrated Books

Every autumn, yet another batch of large, lavish picture books of gardening is published to catch the Christmas trade. Most are coffee-table gift books which will be glanced at, left about for a month or two, and never read again, but a few have lasting quality. One of these is *The English Garden*, a long essay on garden styles by Edward Hyams with photographs of the great gardens of England by Edwin Smith which are among the most beautiful garden photographs I have ever seen. As gardens must necessarily grow and change, so splendid a record of gardens like Bodnant and Sissinghurst in their prime is of the utmost value.

An even more lavish production is *The Dictionary of Garden Plants in Colour*, by Roy Hay and Patrick Synge, one of the most popular gardening books ever published. With 2,048 colour photographs of plants, it is a *tour de force*, and with such distinguished authors, you know the written facts are beyond reproach. The layout and typography are a joy, but I find some of the plant photographs off-colour. For impressions of the garden scene, photography is certainly the supreme medium, but for plant identification, I think botanical drawings are better. This is why I like *Shrubs in Colour* so much, by A. G. L. Hellyer, and the book on wild flowers by the dear old clergyman, the Reverend Keble Martin, who illustrated *The Concise British Flora in Colour* with over 1,000 of his own sketches.

Growers' Catalogues

You will want something besides books in your gardening library. The best catalogues are much more than lists of goods for sale; they are encyclopaedias in their own field. They give growing instructions and cautionary hints about plants which need special protection or treatment or which don't care for lime.

Hillier's *Manual of Trees and Shrubs* is in a class by itself, a classic consulted by connoisseurs all over the world. *The Planter's Handbook*, by George Jackman of Woking, is another excellent list with generous instructions, and John Scott of Merriott, Somerset, have a catalogue illustrated with charming botanical drawings; the list includes many species roses and unusual plants. Thompson and Morgan issue the acknowledged top catalogue for seeds; De Jager for bulbs; Broadleigh Gardens for small bulbs; Perry's Hardy Plant Farm for water plants and ferns; Will Ingwersen Ltd for alpine and rock garden plants. Also to be recommended are the catalogues of Sherrard's Nurseries for shrubs; the Sunningdale Nurseries list for herbaceous plants and shrub roses; the Treasures of Tenbury list for clematis; Thomas Carlile's list for unusual herbaceous plants; John Mattock for roses; Beth Chatto for unusual herbs and foliage plants; Bressingham Gardens for the herbaceous border; and Notcutts' catalogue for a grand sweep of the whole horticultural field.

I have spent many happy Walter Mitty hours by the fire on a January evening surrounded by these catalogues, which I always keep up to date, and with others picked up at the R.H.S. flower shows.

Expensive and Rare Books

If you want to read a book but not necessarily to buy it, because it's too expensive or out of print, the obvious thing is to use the Royal Horticultural Society Lindley Library. You can't buy anything in Great Britain which is better value than a subscription to the R.H.S., which includes use of the peaceful, well-stocked library in Vincent Square, so well looked after by Mr P. Stageman. Many of the books can be sent to members by post, and the reference books and the rarer books can be read in the library itself, which is a few steps from the New Hall where the fortnightly shows are held.

For permanent acquisition, out-of-print books can often be found secondhand. Various bookshops specialize in gardening books, notably, Wheldon & Wesley, Lytton Lodge, Codicote, Hitchin, Herts, and Daniel Lloyd, Heather Lea, 4 Hillcrest Avenue, Chertsey, Surrey. These firms will look out for the books you want, and, if you put your name on the waiting list, they may even get you the great Mr Bowles in due course.

Index

Bracketed spans of page numbers refer to pages between which illustrations will be found.